HOW WOULD JESUS LEAD
WORSHIP?

Text copyright © Sam and Sara Hargreaves 2009
The authors assert the moral right
to be identified as the authors of this work

Published by
The Bible Reading Fellowship
15 The Chambers, Vineyard
Abingdon OX14 3FE
United Kingdom
Tel: +44 (0)1865 319700
Email: enquiries@brf.org.uk
Website: www.brf.org.uk

ISBN 978 1 84101 615 3
First published 2009
10 9 8 7 6 5 4 3 2 1 0
All rights reserved

Acknowledgments
Unless otherwise stated, scripture quotations are taken from the Holy Bible, New International
Version, copyright © 1973, 1978, 1984 by International Bible Society, and are used by
permission of Hodder & Stoughton Publishers, a division of Hodder Headline Ltd. All rights
reserved. 'NIV' is a registered trademark of International Bible Society. UK trademark number
1448790.

Scripture quotations taken from The Holy Bible, Today's New International Version. Copyright ©
2004 by International Bible Society. Used by permission of Hodder & Stoughton, a division of
Hodder Headline Ltd. All rights reserved. 'TNIV' is a registered trademark of International Bible
Society.

Scripture quotations from THE MESSAGE. Copyright © by Eugene H. Peterson 1993, 1994, 1995.
Used by permission of NavPress Publishing Group.

Scripture quotations marked (NLT) are taken from the Holy Bible, New Living Translation,
copyright © 1996, 2004. Used by permission of Tyndale House Publishers, Inc., Wheaton,
Illinois 60189. All rights reserved.

Scripture quotations taken from The New Revised Standard Version of the Bible, Anglicized
Edition, copyright © 1989, 1995 by the Division of Christian Education of the National Council
of the Churches of Christ in the United States of America, are used by permission. All rights
reserved.

A catalogue record for this book is available from the British Library

Printed in Singapore by Craft Print International Ltd

HOW WOULD JESUS LEAD
WORSHIP?

Biblical insights for today's church

SAM AND SARA HARGREAVES

ACKNOWLEDGEMENTS

This book, in many ways, exists thanks to all the generous people who have encouraged, supported and trained us over the years in our journey of worship leading. We would like to thank the staff and students at London School of Theology from 1999 to 2002 for challenging and shaping our thinking and practice of worship, especially David Peacock for mentoring Sam in the years following our graduation.

A huge debt of gratitude is owed to Ascension Church, Balham Hill. Our vicars Stephen Hance and Nikki Groarke believed in us, trusting us to develop innovative forms of worship and outreach, pushing us to go deeper and broader. The worship, creative and youth teams we led were a constant source of inspiration and encouragement, and many of the ideas in this book stem from collaborations with Chloe Axford, Becky Johnson, Suzy Brech, Sam Jones, Beth Reid and many others. For reading the first draft of this book and feeding back great critique, ideas and encouragement, we would like to thank Chris Jack, Heidi Longworth, Matt Osgood, Roger Peach, David Peacock, Phil Barnard and Ruth Neve. Also thanks to Ruth for permission to use her Covenant Feast Communion liturgy in Appendix 2. We are grateful to Bert Ingelsten at Missionskolan, Örebro, Sweden, for the conversation and use of their library.

This book would genuinely have not been possible without the generous provision of accommodation for our sabbatical in Sweden and Peterborough by Paul and Ruth Hine, Paul and Rosemary Jobson, and our parents Sue and John Hargreaves and Claes and Gunilla Johansson. Heartfelt thanks also go to our editor, Naomi Starkey, at BRF for championing this project.

As we look to the future, we are very grateful to St James', Hemingford Grey, for employing Sam to develop worship in our new home, and to the Music and Worship Foundation for commissioning us to begin Engage—equipping youth, young adults and 21st-century churches for innovative worship. To find out more about our resources and training days, visit www.engageworship.org.

CONTENTS

✛

FOREWORD

As a keen observer of the worship scene, I have come to the conclusion that we are currently in a bit of an 'Emperor's new clothes' situation. The festivals continue to thrive; sales of worship CDs and MP3 downloads look healthy enough. And yet, when I talk to *people* I constantly find myself having conversations about how worship has become boring or predictable, and how it 'doesn't do it for me any more'. The grand parade continues, but more and more people seem to be spotting the naked truth.

Sam and Sara, leaders of *Engage*, the youthful offspring of the Music and Worship Foundation, address this issue, refreshingly beginning with theology. They look hard at two of the major Christian doctrines, Incarnation and Trinity, and at Luke's Gospel through 'worship' lenses, and while presupposing and connecting with the evangelical/charismatic worship-song culture they give a *cri de coeur* for the church to move on from mere singing, from self-indulgence and sameness. Not just a *cri de coeur*, though, because they also give us all kinds of practical ideas, worship experiences to try, resources to explore, and a helpful process by which we can more effectively plan our worship services.

If there is one message that I believe the Spirit is currently trying to get through to the church, it has to do with whole-life Christianity: God is crying out for faith that is lived out, faith that is there to be a blessing as well as to be blessed, less concerned with the services we hold than with the service we give, and for worship that has this flavour too. This book helps us to know exactly how to begin to do it.

How would Jesus write a book on worship leading? Maybe just like this. Enjoy!

John Leach, Parish Development Adviser, Monmouth Diocese, and Executive Director, Music and Worship Foundation

✠

PART 1

INTRODUCTION

Can you imagine it? There's a hush of anticipation among the assembled crowd. The lights dim, and then comes an announcement over the PA:

'Ladies and gentlemen, we are pleased to have with us tonight possibly the most anointed worship leader ever. Please welcome: Jesus Christ!'

The crowd goes wild as the young man with boyish good looks straps on his acoustic guitar and the band kicks into one of the bigger hits from his many CDs.

Can you imagine it? Is this the image that comes into your mind if someone says, 'Jesus, the worship leader'? Or let's narrow it down: what mental associations does the word 'worship' conjure up for you? Times of singing with optional hand-raising for the keen; acoustic guitars, with or without the rainbow straps; organs, choirs and dog collars; hymn/prayer sandwiches?

Through the last few generations, trends in Christian worship have changed many times. In some ways, it is just like the changing fashions in clothing and hairstyles: as the bell-bottom trousers shifted to the drainpipe, so the modern hymn was ditched for the repeated chorus, before being upstaged by the longer worship song. Just as the way we dress expresses something of who we are, our values and personalities, so worship styles seek to express something of our take on God, in musical styles that we hope will relate to the world around us.

We may well know people who have chosen a clothing style from a particular period and stuck with it. Churches and individuals often pick a worship style from a certain era and stop moving with the trends. Others attempt to be eclectic in their approach and draw from different 'looks', running the risk of ending up with the worship equivalent of a top hat, a Mickey Mouse T-shirt, a sarong and Ugg boots. Still others will be constantly moving on, always using the very latest songs, their technology getting flashier, their presentation more and more professional.

Are any of these approaches wrong in themselves? Of course not. The problem comes when we start thinking, or even saying, that our style is 'the one'. Imagine someone saying to you, 'The only godly way to dress is in a formal suit', or 'Deuteronomy clearly states that we must dress in all different kinds of styles, to relate to people from all walks of life', or 'Jesus would keep up with the trends—we must be completely up to date with what we wear'. It sounds ridiculous, but we do this with worship. We elevate one style and find 'biblical' or 'pastoral' reasons to justify our choice. We could, of course, be honest and admit that it's more to do with our personal preferences and, perhaps, our image of God.

Want to dress like Jesus? Get a one-piece linen garment. And some sandals. No socks.

Want to sing like Jesus? Take a course in everyday Aramaic and learn some ancient Near Eastern scales and harmonies.

Want to *worship* like Jesus? Now we are asking a very different question, one that's less to do with style, and more to do with heart, attitude and the working of the Holy Spirit.

This book invites you to test your worship style—your expression of worship—against the ultimate worshipper. Sure, your style is an expression of who you are, but it should also be subject to the Bible's values and parameters for worship. We hope that this book will help you discover the core of what it means to be a worshipper, perhaps a worship leader. And at the end of it all, we hope that Jesus will inspire your worship so that it is rooted in Christ-like attitudes towards God, one another, the community you are trying to reach and the wider world that God so loves.

I'LL BRING YOU MORE THAN A SONG...

Before we go any further, let's look at one key issue. There is a serious problem in Western evangelical/charismatic churches to do with the terms 'worship' and 'worship leader'. Many church leaders will assure you that 'of course, worship is so much more than singing'. Yet do we model this belief in practice? For most Christians, does a 'time of worship' mean anything more than a time of singing? Most people assume that a worship leader does nothing more than lead church music, so if the 'worship leader' only leads the singing, then 'worship' must just be singing.

This thinking reflects only a small part of the biblical picture of worship. When we see the word 'worship' in the Bible, we are actually reading a translation of a number of different, interconnected words. For example, the 'worship' of Jesus as described in Luke 24:52 is a translation of *proskynein*, a word meaning 'homage' or 'reverence'. In Acts 13:2, however, where we read of the Antioch church 'worshipping', the Greek verb is *leitourgein*, which is linked more to a religious service, like our word 'liturgy'.[1] Also, word studies alone are not enough, because the Bible often talks about the concept or practice of worship without using the term 'worship'. It is important to step back and take a look at the big picture.

While it would certainly be possible to argue other variations and additions to the following, this is our best summary of the biblical perspective on worship.

- Worship is about reverently drawing near to God.
- Worship is being obedient in service to God's design for our lives.

- Worship is offering God the praise and glory that he alone deserves.

We were created to worship God in this way—to live in close relationship with him, to serve him and his world, and to give him praise and glory. It is vital to note that the Bible gives equal importance to these things being lived out in people's everyday lives and being expressed in acts of corporate worship. The patriarchs, the prophets, Jesus and the early Church leaders had an equal concern that the people of God should be worshipping with their lifestyles, relationships, work, finances, attitudes towards the poor and so on (see Deuteronomy 26:12–13; Amos 5:23–24; Matthew 5:23–24; Romans 12:1) *and* that their worship should be expressed in songs, prayers and other symbolic acts as they met together (1 Chronicles 15:16–22; Isaiah 12:4–6; Mark 14:22–26; 1 Corinthians 14:26). Hebrews 13:15–16 is a great example of this equal concern, as in one breath the writer encourages the people to worship God through Jesus with their lips, and at the same time to remember to do good and share with others. As THE MESSAGE puts it, 'God takes particular pleasure in acts of worship—a different kind of "sacrifice"—that take place in kitchen and workplace and on the streets' (13:16).

The problem for much of the church today is that we have managed to separate these two facets of worship—worship as lived out in daily life and worship as corporate gathering. Somehow we have pushed them even further apart, so that for some believers the only point of the corporate gathering is the chance for individuals to meet with God through a narrow selection of worship songs. We rightly concentrate on praising God and drawing near to him in intimate adoration, but we do so at the expense of many other important facets to our worship life. This can lead to criticisms of evangelical/charismatic worship as being individualized to the point of selfishness, spiritualized to the point of complete separation from everyday life, and formulaic to the point of boredom.

How can we escape these pitfalls and find a model for authentic worship? When Soul Survivor church in Watford stripped back their musical worship for a season, it inspired Matt Redman to write this song, which has inspired many people to rethink their worship.

I'll bring you more than a song, for a song in itself
is not what you have required.
You search much deeper within, through the way things appear,
you're looking into my heart.
I'm coming back to the heart of worship,
and it's all about you, all about you, Jesus. [2]

MATT REDMAN, COPYRIGHT © 1997 THANKYOU MUSIC

This exceptional song points us towards Jesus as the true heart of worship. In him we see one who fulfils our threefold definition of worship perfectly: drawing near to God the Father, being obedient to his will and glorifying him, both in his everyday life and in his specific acts of corporate worship, such as singing (Matthew 26:30), prayer (Luke 10:21) and symbolic action (22:17–23). This book explores whether, in the light of the life of Jesus, our services have indeed defined worship too narrowly, and whether people other than musicians could rightly be called worship leaders. Dare we ask Jesus to show us a deeper way, where our gathered times of worship become a concentrated expression of lives lived in close relationship with God, serving in obedience to his will, to his praise and glory?

BACKGROUND TO THIS BOOK

The thinking behind this book first began to take shape when we both took the London School of Theology *Theology, Music and Worship* degree course. [3] Here we learned to fuse our deepening understanding of God, his word and his people with our practice of leading people in worship. While we built up our musical skills and enjoyed some amazing times of singing praise to God, we also began to experience worship as much more than just singing, and theology as far more than just 'what the Greek says'. We found worship and theology together offering the way to a life-giving adventure, going deeper with God.

In particular, Sam's provocatively titled dissertation 'Jesus is my girlfriend?' really helped to spark our thinking about Jesus and worship. The paper addressed a particular fad in worship songs where the writer tries to express intimacy with God by using the human language of romantic love: 'in your arms I lie', 'closer than lovers', 'I'm falling in love with you' and so forth. It concluded that while the language was more influenced by pop songs than by the Bible and was probably unhelpful, the intention of expressing intimacy with God was a right and biblical one.[4] In Jesus' life on earth we see the most intimate relationship with Father God. Graham Kendrick expressed it like this in an email interview for the dissertation:

The supreme example of worship intimacy surely has to be looked for in Christ Jesus and his relationship with the Father, from Jesus' baptism when the Father spoke over him the words 'This is my beloved Son with whom I am well pleased', through to the drama of Gethsemane where Jesus' love is proved by his obedience even to the point of death on a cross: 'Not my will, but yours.'[5]

Writing the dissertation got us thinking about two key interlinked topics—big, daunting, yet life-giving theological concepts that blew our minds and revolutionized our worship. Firstly, in the doctrine of the incarnation, the earthly life of Christ, we see the fully human Jesus living as the ultimate worshipper. Secondly, in the doctrine of the Trinity we see how we can be drawn in by the Holy Spirit to share in the intimate relationship that the incarnate Jesus has with God the Father. James Torrance's book *Worship, Community and the Triune God of Grace* stirred us with its central theme, that 'worship and the mission of the Church are the gift of participating through the Holy Spirit in the incarnate Son's communion with the Father'.[6]

Suddenly worship was more than songs, words and music. It was about being drawn into the most amazing relationship ever. Jesus, by the Spirit, was the true worship leader, making the way clear for us to draw near to our Father.

Theories turn to practice

This was good in theory, and we had the opportunity to test it out a bit in college chapels and other events. Then we moved to Ascension, Balham Hill, a local Anglican church in South London. Here we had the challenge and the privilege of developing worship around the theories we had been nurturing at college. We wrote songs that attempted to involve people in the trinitarian dynamic of worship.[7] We preached on it. We centred our worship team on the vision 'To lead worship as Jesus leads worship'.

We discussed as a team how this vision had two levels of meaning. Firstly, Jesus was the only one whom we could truly call our worship leader—the one who lived a perfect life of worship and opened the way for us to join with him in praising the Father and entering into his presence, by the Spirit. (This meaning is unpacked in Chapter 1 of this book.) Secondly, we agreed that 'to lead worship as Jesus leads worship' also meant that we should look to Jesus as our role model and inspiration for worship leading. We challenged each other to read the Gospels with fresh eyes, asking how Jesus' attitudes and actions could be applied to church worship. The second part of this book, Chapters 2 to 5, explores the wristband slogan 'What would Jesus do?' in relation to worship. As one of our college lecturers was fond of saying, before you ask 'What would Jesus do?' you need to find out what Jesus *did* do. So we studied the Gospel of Luke, with commentaries open and brains switched on, working to understand the context and the original language. We focused on relating the Gospel teachings to our experiences of leading worship in church and other contexts. Most importantly, we tried to come to the text with a prayerful attitude, letting it challenge our own lives and practice of worship. At times, as we did this, we were led to our knees in repentance, and many more times we took to our feet or instruments in worship as God showed us more of himself.

Our findings, as laid out in this book, are organized around four key points, used as chapter headings, which we have found useful in helping us encapsulate our ponderings. These are definitions of Jesus (and, potentially, each worship leader) as:

- Humble servant
- Leader with authority
- Creative communicator
- Reliant on the Spirit

Now, we want to make it very clear that these are just our personal conclusions, after prayerfully studying Luke through the lens of worship. You will probably come up with some different thoughts and categories. In fact, we very much hope you will. We are certainly not claiming that our thoughts, however well researched, tested or discussed, are the complete picture. We ourselves are on a journey, exploring how the life of Jesus might influence us as worship leaders and applying our finding to the context in which we find ourselves. Our aim is to spark questions, provoke debate and inspire study.

HOLDING TENSIONS

Have you ever shot with a bow and arrow? You put the arrow in the correct position, hold the bow in one hand and the string in the other, and pull one hand as far from the other as you can. It can feel a bit worrying, especially if the bow is old: what if either wood or string breaks? Yet it is exactly that tension, created between bow and string, that gives power and energy to the arrow and provides you with that unbeatable Robin Hood 'twang'.

Although we might try to avoid it, tension is actually a hugely important creative force. Tension in a movie is what keeps the plot moving along. Tensions created by suspensions and cadences are what give shape to music. Even tuning an instrument like a piano, guitar or drum kit is an exercise in tension—pulling one thing against another to create a resonant, pleasing noise.

Good theology is often the act of holding ideas in tension. For example, in Chapter 1 we talk about the incarnation. When the early Church needed to formulate biblical truth into doctrine to avoid misunderstanding and heresy, they had to hold together two apparently opposite truths—that the incarnate Jesus was (and is) both fully God and fully human. We also talk, in Chapter 2, about the Trinity—one God, three persons. We may hope for a nice easy metaphor to explain what this really means but the creeds do not allow us to collapse the tension, and, the more we delve into it, the more we will find that it gives us life.

Many of our problems to do with worship in the Western church come from the collapse of tensions that should be held and celebrated. For example, either we choose the transcendence of God, focusing on his power and majesty, or we cosy up to the immanent, intimate God, majoring on his love and grace. Yet these attributes are supposed to be pulling against one another all the time, as we proclaim and experience our God who is holy and beyond us, yet makes himself known and available through his Son and Spirit.

How about the tension between reaching seekers with easy-access gospel presentations (spiritual milk: Hebrews 5:13) and taking believers deeper in teaching and worship (spiritual meat: v. 14)? Or the choice between hymns, with their depth of lyrical content but often low cultural relevance, and the contemporary but sometimes thematically lightweight choruses? The 'we' of corporate worship versus the 'I' of personal response? Planned versus spontaneous? Quiet reflection versus noisy celebration?[8]

In Jesus, we see someone who does not fall for the temptation to collapse tensions. For example, he knows that his kingdom is not of this world (John 18:36), yet he makes a difference to people in the world (Luke 7:22). He came to save the whole of humankind, yet has time to stop with one individual (seen when he speaks with one penitent thief while dying on the cross for the whole world: Luke 23:40–43). He is the Lord of lords, yet he came to serve (Matthew 20:28). His yoke is easy and his burden is light (11:30), yet he takes up his cross and calls us to do the same (16:24).

Looking at the life of Jesus as a guide and model for our worship has helped us to see that we can often make false choices, narrowing down our worship style or practice to please ourselves or our congregations, when in fact Jesus calls us to hold styles in tension and celebrate the difference. The book's chapter headings pull against each other in very important ways: we are to follow Jesus' example in being 'humble servants' of our congregations and our communities, and at the same time we are called to be 'leaders with authority'. This might sound impossible, but Jesus shows us how. We are to develop our 'creative communication', planning and rehearsing music, arts and other worship experiences fit for a king, and yet at the same time be 'reliant on the Spirit', not our own gifts, being adaptable and ready to change our plans at his leading. Jesus takes what is humanly impossible and shows how, with God, all things are possible (Matthew 19:26).

HOW TO USE THIS BOOK

As already stated, there are two main sections to this book. Chapter 1 deals with the theory and theology of how we might understand Jesus as our worship leader, based on the book of Hebrews, considering the implications of the incarnation and the doctrine of the Trinity. Part 2, Chapters 2 to 5, is more practical, dealing with the way in which principles from Jesus' life as found in Luke's Gospel influence our worship leading today.

Throughout the book, there are practical examples putting the various ideas into practice in corporate worship. The end of Part 1 presents a number of ideas as to how the theology can be applied in services. 'Leader with authority' talks about how worship can be planned, and the importance of journey, thinking through overall aims, not just the choice of music. 'Creative communicator' is brimming with creative ideas for how to move worship beyond simply singing, and 'Humble servants' looks at how we can fuse worship with social action.

You might find it helpful to study this book with your worship group, home group or other like-minded friends. If you do this, we suggest that you choose a chunk to look at each time you meet, read it before you get together, but then come with your Bibles to discuss not only our thoughts but also what you get out of the passages. We often ask questions such as 'Do you do things like that in your church?' and these can be pointers for discussion or individual reflection.

We also want your experience of this book to be an act of worship in itself, so the heading 'Worship experience' is an invitation to put the book down and do some kind of activity to respond to God. These activities could also be helpful to try together if you are reading the book as a group. It can be tempting to skip this kind of thing when you read a book (we know!), but give it a try and we pray that you will experience drawing closer to God. In fact, here is the first 'Worship experience' to finish this introduction. Go for it!

 WORSHIP EXPERIENCE

If it's possible, go to a public place where you can see people. Look out of your window or sit on a bench in a park or near to some shops. Look at the people passing by and think about who they might be, what their lives might be like. Do they look happy or sad? Do they seem excited, tired, nervous or bored?

Does anyone appear to be in pain? Are they with friends, with family or alone?

Now consider the people in the first chapter of Luke's Gospel. They were real, flesh-and-blood people: Zechariah, the priest—old and alone; his wife, Elizabeth—past her best, shamed in a society that valued women for their fertility; their relative, Mary—young, poor and frightened. Do you know people who are like them? Can you see anyone around you who reminds you of them?

In what ways are you like Zechariah, Elizabeth or Mary? Are you considered too old or too young to make a difference, perhaps in leading worship? Have you been shunned or shamed? Are you seen as a failure, by others or by yourself?

Hear God's messenger speak to these people of flesh and blood:

'Do not be afraid, Zechariah; your prayer has been heard. Your wife Elizabeth will bear you a son, and you are to give him the name John... And he will go on before the Lord, in the spirit and power of Elijah, to turn the hearts of the parents to their children and the disobedient to the wisdom of the righteous—to make ready a people prepared for the Lord' (Luke 1:13, 17).

'Do not be afraid, Mary, you have found favour with God. You will be with child and give birth to a son, and you are to give him the name Jesus. He will be great and will be called the Son of the Most High. The Lord God will give him the throne of his father David, and he will reign over the house of Jacob forever; his kingdom will never end' (vv. 30–33).

Can you hear a message from God to you echo down through the generations? Remember: 'you are a chosen people, a royal priesthood, a holy nation, a people belonging to God' (1 Peter 2:9). You are chosen, like Zechariah, Elizabeth and Mary.

Notice, too, that it's OK to have fears and questions: "'How will this be," Mary asked the angel, "since I am a virgin?"' (Luke 1:34). What are your questions for God about his calling on your life? What are your fears about how that calling might work out? What aspects of being involved in leading worship cause you self-doubt or worry? Write them down or speak them out to God. He is gracious and he will listen.

While we can admit our fears and questions, we can pray that we will arrive at Mary's state of heart: "'I am the Lord's servant," Mary answered. "May it be to me as you have said"' (v. 38). We can pray that, in the midst of our questions, we will rise up again to worship the God who chooses the small people:

And Mary said: 'My soul glorifies the Lord and my spirit rejoices in God my Saviour, for he has been mindful of the humble state of his servant. From now on all generations will call me blessed, for the Mighty One has done great things for me—holy is his name. His mercy extends to those who fear him, from generation to generation' (vv. 46–50).

A NOTE ABOUT COPYRIGHT

In this book we suggest playing CDs and film clips in church. At the time of writing, you do not need a licence to play recorded music in a time of worship but you do need a Church Video Licence to play films. Information is available from www.ccli.co.uk, where you can also purchase licences.

✛

Chapter 1

JESUS IS MY WORSHIP LEADER?

He gave some to be apostles, some to be prophets, some to be evangelists, and some to be pastors and teachers, some to be worship leaders...

Actually, the New Testament doesn't say that, but sometimes we may wish that it did. Try as we might, we won't find a specific role or spiritual gift described that covers what we know as 'worship leader' today. In one sense, that is not a problem. There is no mention of 'children's worker' or 'caretaker' either, but we are quite happy to accept these roles as part of contemporary church life. But it gets more tricky when we start to question what the role of 'worship leader' actually entails from a biblical point of view, and even more confusing if someone suggests that Jesus is, in fact, the ultimate worship leader. Theologian James Torrance wrote:

Jesus Christ is the leader of our worship, and leads us into the holy presence of the Father... He is the one true Priest, the one true worshipper, the leader of our worship, in whom alone the 'ordinances of worship' are perfectly fulfilled and through whom alone we can draw near to God. [1]

If the term 'worship leader' isn't even found in the Bible, how can Torrance suggest that Jesus perfectly fulfils it? His key inspiration is the book of Hebrews, a part of the New Testament that, at first glance, might seem tricky, with all its talk of sacrifice, tabernacles and some chap called Melchizedek. The more we delve into this book of the Bible, however, the more we find that the anonymous writer is passionate about worship, and the fact that Jesus is the centre of it all: 'Through Jesus, therefore, let us continually offer to God a sacrifice of praise—the fruit of lips that confess his name' (13:15).[2]

Hebrews explores how Jesus is the fulfilment of Old Testament worship, which was centred on the sacrificial system and was led not primarily by the musicians but by the priests.[3] These were the people set aside by God to offer the true worship of sacrifices and offerings from the people to God.[4]

The first time we read about the sacrificial system in the Old Testament, we may well wonder what on earth is going on—animal sacrifices, sprinkling blood, strange rituals, they all sound very alien to our way of life today. It's a bit like visiting a castle or some other historical building, full of apparently archaic, unfamiliar objects. Have you ever visited a place like that and then met a helpful tour guide, who brings the whole place to life with amusing stories, fascinating facts and a passion for how it all relates to life today? The central chapters of the book of Hebrews are a bit like a helpful guided tour of the Old Testament system, bringing it to life for us. They show how Jesus fulfils all that God set up for worship in that first covenant and goes beyond it to allow everybody access to worship their heavenly Father God. But let's begin with the bad news...

WHENEVER WE COME TO WORSHIP, WE SHOULD DIE

When God created humanity, his plan was always for us to worship him and live in his presence. We established in the Introduction that worship is, in part, about reverently drawing near to God. As we know from Genesis 3 and our own experience, however, human selfishness broke that relationship and made us unholy. One of the central problems of Old Testament worship is this: if an unholy people come into contact with the holy God, the result can only be certain death (Exodus 33:20; Leviticus 10:1–3; 1 Chronicles 13:9–10).[5]

We could think of sin as being a bit like the outbreak of Foot and Mouth disease that caused havoc a few years back: the only way to stop it was to slaughter and burn all the affected animals. We are 'infected' by the disease of sin, which leads to death (Romans 5:12). God's holiness is a 'consuming fire' (Hebrews 12:29), obliterating any unholiness it encounters. This could make worship difficult (to say the least!). Would many people be attracted to our churches if certain death was on the order of service, just after the notices?

In the light of this, we can see that all the rules and sacrifices of the Old Testament system were God's way of protecting his people. He set up the tabernacle, and later the temple, with physical barriers between himself and the people, to save them from being obliterated by his holy presence. Hebrews explains how this set-up looked.

Now the first covenant had regulations for worship and also an earthly sanctuary. A tabernacle was set up. In its first room were the lampstand, the table and the consecrated bread; this was called the Holy Place. Behind the second curtain was a room called the Most Holy Place, which had the golden altar of incense and the gold-covered ark of the covenant... Above the ark were the cherubim of the Glory, overshadowing the atonement cover (9:1–5).

This passage describes the tabernacle, the sacred space that God provided as a means for his people to come and worship him. There was an outer court, where the ordinary people could come. Then there was the Holy Place, where the priests could go to offer sacrifices. Finally, behind a thick curtain, was the Most Holy Place, or Holy of Holies, where God's presence on earth hovered above the ark of the covenant.

Leviticus 16:2 holds a severe warning for Aaron, the first high priest: 'Tell your brother Aaron not to come whenever he chooses into the Most Holy Place behind the curtain in front of the atonement cover on the ark, or else he will die, because I appear in the cloud over the atonement cover.' Leviticus 16 goes on to explain how the high priest is to enter the Most Holy Place once a year, on the Day of Atonement, to offer two goats for the sins of the people (v. 7). It wasn't even straightforward for him to go in there: first a bull had to be sacrificed to make him clean (v. 6), there were sacred clothes for him to wear (v. 4), and he had to burn incense, whose smoke would hide him from the presence of God and protect him from being struck down (vv. 12–13).

Knowing this, it should shock us, as it must have profoundly shocked the first readers, to see the writer to the Hebrews say:

Therefore, brothers and sisters, since we have confidence to enter the Most Holy Place by the blood of Jesus, *by a new and living way opened for us through the curtain, that is, his body, and since we have a* great priest *over the house of God, let us* draw near to God *with a sincere heart in full assurance of faith, having our hearts sprinkled to cleanse us from a guilty conscience and having our bodies washed with pure water* (10:19–22, emphasis added).

What? Entering the Most Holy Place means death! We can't go beyond that curtain; even the high priest could only do that once a year. We dare not draw so close to God: we are unholy, he is holy. 'Yes, you can,' says our writer, and Jesus gives us two very important reasons why. Firstly, his blood, shed for us on the cross, opened up a new and living way into God's presence, far superior to the blood of the goat on the Day of Atonement. Secondly, we have a new high priest, one who is far superior to Aaron and his sons, who offered the sacrifice of his blood for us. Jesus takes the role of both sacrifice and high priest, uniquely offering himself as the once-for-all solution to the problem of sin. As F.F. Bruce writes, 'In the death of Jesus, we are to understand, God himself is unveiled to us and the way of access to him is thrown wide open.'[6]

It is all too easy to be casual and glib about coming into God's presence in worship, forgetting that we can do so only because we have been saved from death. Before we move on, it is worth taking a moment to reflect on Luke 23:44–46, where we read that, at the moment Jesus died, the curtain separating us from the Holy of Holies, the very presence of God, was torn in two from top to bottom. The way was made open for each one of us, however sinful and unworthy, to enter not a room in a tent or a temple but the heavenly reality of which the Old Testament system was only a picture—coming into the presence of our loving Father.

Spend some time pondering this amazing fact, the wonder of what Jesus has done for us. The next question to ask might be, 'How is this possible?' What is it about Jesus that makes him uniquely qualified to make this happen, in a way that the previous system could only hint at? In answering this question, we will encounter two vital cornerstones of our faith: the incarnation and the Trinity.

THE INCARNATION

The writer to the Hebrews uses the image of the Old Testament high priest to show how Jesus' coming to earth as a human makes a difference for us. He explains: 'Every high priest is selected from among the people and is appointed to represent them in matters related to God, to offer gifts and sacrifices for sins. He is able to deal gently with those who are ignorant and are going astray, since he himself is subject to weakness' (5:1–2, TNIV).

Remember, the high priest was the closest figure in the Old Testament to a worship leader. He was the representative of God's people in their worship. Like an ambassador or a mediator, he acted as a go-between, while being aware of his own humanity and weakness. Jesus had to become fully human in order to take on the role of high priest. It is an ancient yet enduring heresy that Jesus was just pretending to be human, as if he wore human clothes and bumbled around like Clark Kent, yet under it all he was really a kind of Superman.

The writer to the Hebrews is deeply concerned that we should not make this mistake. The Christian faith has always affirmed that the incarnate Jesus was fully God and yet also fully human—one of those creative tensions that we described in the Introduction. We need to hold tight to both Jesus' humanity and his divinity, not choosing one over the other but allowing them to pull against each other and shape our understanding of him. As Hebrews says, 'We do not have a high priest who is unable to sympathize with our weaknesses, but we have one who has been tempted in every way, just as we are—yet was without sin' (4:15).

Born a human being just like us, Jesus faced the same temptations that we do. He took on our fallen humanity, with the genuine potential that he could have sinned—and yet he did not do so. Part of our definition of worship is 'being obedient in service to God's design for our lives'. Jesus is the perfect example of somebody entirely devoted to living the Father's will (John 5:36). He shows us what it means to be fully human, fully alive, focused completely in worship of God. Thus Ron Man, director of Worship Resources International (www. worr.org), can say of him, 'In Jesus Christ as perfect man God has likewise found the true worshipper, the man who can truly approach God on his own merits, with a completely pure heart and conscience (Ps. 15:1–2) and offer up worthy praise.'[7]

The writer to the Hebrews quotes Psalm 40 to show how living this fully human yet obedient and sinless life made Jesus uniquely qualified to die in our place:

First he said, 'Sacrifices and offerings, burnt offerings and sin offerings you did not desire, nor were you pleased with them' (although the law required them to be made). Then he said, 'Here I am, I have come to do your will.' He sets aside the first to establish the second. And by that will, we have been made holy through the sacrifice of the body of Jesus Christ once and for all (10:8–10).

What the writer is saying is that the blood of bulls and goats could not save people fully: God provided the sacrificial system only as a temporary means for the Israelites to come to him. It could not provide lasting purification of body and soul (9:9, 13; 10:3–4). In the end, humanity had to die for its own sin, and yet, as sinful beings, we could not be the spotless sacrifice that was required. Only Jesus, by living the Father's will as a perfect human being, could take our place. On the cross, his sacrifice dealt with death for ever and made us holy. His life of perfect worship makes worship possible for us.

In recognizing the significance of Jesus' humanity, we should take a fresh look at our church services. We may tend to sing only about the risen, exalted Jesus, while neglecting to celebrate his earthly life. If Jesus' humanity was real, genuine flesh and blood, then he was born with the same weakness and need for teaching and development that are common to us all (Luke 2:41–52). His hunger and thirst would have been genuine (Matthew 21:18; John 19:28). He would have got properly tired (John 4:6). Jesus affirms the essential goodness of our humanity, redeemed and made perfect in him. Gathered worship in this context should be not only focused on the heavenlies but also rooted in our everyday lives. Have you been involved in worship that celebrates our human experiences in the light of Jesus? Do we offer people the comfort that Jesus knows what it is like to be human, to struggle, to be tempted?

Sara once preached on Jesus' humanity in an all-age service and needed a song as a response for the congregation. Sam wrote one for the occasion and it has become one of our favourite all-age songs.[8] The verse that goes, 'Jesus, you know what it's like to be lonely, tired and hungry, excited and clumsy...' has given us much comfort, as it provides a basic description of our lives! Engaging with Jesus' humanity is a largely untapped source of encouragement for congregations, and an area where we fail to give Jesus full credit and glory.

THE TRINITY

So far, we have looked at how Jesus solved for all time the problem that unholy people were unable to come into the presence of God, by offering himself, as both sacrifice and high priest, on the cross. We have seen that part of the reason why Jesus was uniquely qualified to do so was that he lived a fully human life of obedient worship. But what about the fact that he was fully God? What impact does that have on our worship? The writer to the Hebrews addresses this at the very beginning of the letter.

In the past God spoke to our ancestors through the prophets at many times and in various ways, but in these last days he has spoken to us by his Son, whom he appointed heir of all things, and through whom he made the universe. The Son is the radiance of God's glory and the exact representation of God's being, sustaining all things by his powerful word (1:1–3a).

As we can see here, the writer is very concerned to show that Jesus is far more than a prophet or an angel. He speaks of 'his Son', implying that Jesus is God. If you need any more convincing, look at verse 6: 'And again, when God brings his firstborn into the world, he says, "Let all God's angels worship him."'

It may seem quite normal for us to think of Jesus as deserving worship, but it would have been scandalous to the original hearers. Central to Israel's faith was the conviction that God was one (Deuteronomy 6:4) and that no one else could share his worship. As good Jews, Jesus' first followers believed passionately that God was one. They knew that Jesus was not himself the Father. Yet they also knew and worshipped Jesus as God (Matthew 28:17; Luke 24:52). Although they may not have argued over the finer points or written them up as a detailed creed, the New Testament Christians bore witness to Jesus as God, and to the Father as God.

They also began to see the intimate connection between the Father, the Son and a third person, the Holy Spirit. They grasped that the incarnate Jesus was, unlike us, perfectly filled with the Holy Spirit from birth to do the will of the Father. John the Baptist says of him that he has been given 'the Spirit without limit' (John 3:34), and Jesus himself explains that he 'can do nothing by himself; he can do only what he sees his Father doing' (5:19). In his conception, baptism, preaching, miracles, worship and in other points of his earthly life, Jesus was empowered by the Holy Spirit to do the will of the Father.[9] His life and worship are our clearest example of what became known as the doctrine of the Trinity.[10]

Theologian Robert Jenson has called the Trinity—Father, Son, and Holy Spirit—'the proper name of God'.[11] It is the primary way that God has revealed himself to us, so, in one sense, getting to grips with the concept of the Trinity is no more than doing God the courtesy of getting his name right. If focusing on doctrine like this is not your idea of fun, you could think of it like the white lines on a football pitch. They may not appear very important at first, but without them the game loses all shape and structure. The lines make a great match possible. Understanding the Trinity makes great worship possible. More than that, as we worship, we can do far more than just thinking about or understanding the Trinity: we can experience the three-in-one God.

This was how the first Christians began to grasp the concept of one God, as Father, Son and Holy Spirit: they experienced it in their worship and their relationship with God. They drew near to God the Father through the life, death and resurrection of the Son, in the power of the Holy Spirit. And they did this because they had first seen it modelled in the life of Jesus, as he lived in intimate relationship with his Father, by the Holy Spirit.

One example of this intimacy can be seen in Jesus' use of the word *Abba*, a word that, according to scholars, had never been used before by Israelites to refer to God, as it was far too intimate and homely. Jesus, in using it freely, was demonstrating a 'relationship with God of unique intimacy and intensity'.[12]

The truly amazing fact is that we, too, can be filled and empowered by the same Holy Spirit, to worship the Father in the same way that Jesus did: 'Because you are his children, God sent the Spirit of his Son into our hearts, the Spirit who calls out, "Abba, Father"' (Galatians 4:6).

Because of what Jesus has done on the cross, we are adopted by

God as sons and daughters (Ephesians 1:5). God puts his Spirit in our hearts so that, just as Jesus did, we can enter into that intimate relationship, calling God *Abba*, drawing close to our loving heavenly Father. As James Torrance would say, worship is when we join with the Son, in worshipping the Father, by the Spirit. If we are 'in Christ', our worship is offered 'through Christ', and we can know God the Father as Jesus knew him. Our worship becomes far more than singing some songs or saying some words to a distant God who may or may not hear us. It becomes a sharing in the Son's worship and relationship with the Father, by the Spirit.

High priest for ever

We have seen how Jesus solved the problem of an unholy people coming to worship a holy God, by his perfect sacrifice on the cross. He shared the same humanity as the 'worship leaders' of the old covenant, the priests, and yet was without sin. At the same time, Jesus' priesthood is far greater because he is the eternal Son of God; he has been appointed by God as 'priest for ever' of a different priestly order, in a new and better covenant where he continues to serve at the right hand of God in heaven (see Hebrews 8:1–6). The implications for our worship today are profound. Not only has Jesus shown us how to live a life of perfect worship, not only has he made the way for us to worship by his sacrifice, and not only has he invited us to share in his relationship with the Father, but he also continues to offer our praise to the Father right now. To say 'Jesus is our worship leader' means not only that he has opened the way to the Father in the past, but that right now he 'lives to intercede' for us (Hebrews 7:25) as we worship the Father in him, by the Spirit.

We, the people who call ourselves worship leaders, are not the mediators between the people and God. That role belongs to Jesus (1 Timothy 2:5; Hebrews 8:6). It is not up to us to 'make something happen', to create an atmosphere or attempt to generate a response.

It is God who has made the way in Jesus, through the Spirit, to worship him. It is Jesus, by the Spirit, who continues to take our worship and present it to Father God. It is the Spirit who enables us to join with the Son as he glorifies the Father.

This should bring us freedom and encouragement as we take up the privileged role of partnering with Christ, by the Spirit, to lead our congregations in worship. We will never get ourselves 'right' enough to offer sufficient worship to God. No amount of practice, creativity, effort or planning can force a way into the presence of the Father. Yet in his mercy he has made a way: in Christ we can offer acceptable worship by the Spirit. In Jesus, the Father has dealt with the stain of our sin and ripped down the curtains that kept us from entering into the Holy of Holies, his very presence. By his grace he welcomes us into that perfect relationship of love, to join the Son as he perfectly worships the Father in the Spirit.

Worship the worship leader

Before we consider the practical application of all this in the life of the church, we should note a potential pitfall. In thinking about Jesus as worship leader, we can forget that he too is worthy of our worship. The first example from Jesus' earthly life is that he was worshipped by the Magi as a baby (Matthew 2:11), and we have already noted the disciples worshipping him, especially after the resurrection (see Matthew 28:17; Luke 24:52). Although most New Testament prayer and worship is addressed to the Father through the Son (Romans 5:11; Colossians 3:17; 1 Peter 1:3), we do read of the worship of Jesus in the epistles—for example, when Paul says that 'at the name of Jesus every knee should bow' (Philippians 2:10), or when he proclaims that Christ is God and for ever praised (Romans 9:5). In Revelation 5:12–13 we find a glorious picture of Jesus, the Lamb of God, worshipped for eternity along with him who 'sits on the throne', God the Father:

In a loud voice [the angels] sang: 'Worthy is the Lamb, who was slain, to receive power and wealth and wisdom and strength and honour and glory and praise!' Then I heard every creature in heaven and on earth and under the earth and on the sea, and all that is in them, singing: 'To him who sits on the throne and to the Lamb be praise and honour and glory and power, for ever and ever!'

It is part of the tension inherent in the doctrine of the Trinity that the Son and the Spirit act to bring glory to the Father, yet each is also fully God and, as such, is worthy of worship.[13] In recognizing Jesus as the one who leads us to the Father, let us also give him praise and thanks and glory, because that is exactly what he deserves.

 WORSHIP IDEAS

If you are finding all this helpful in your understanding of worship, we would encourage you to think through how you can pass it on to your worship team and the church as a whole. While Bible studies and sermons are obvious ways to communicate these truths, simply letting the trinitarian and incarnational aspects of worship permeate times of corporate praise may have even more of an impact. You may find yourself not only thinking about but also experiencing being drawn in to worship the Father, through the Son, in the Holy Spirit.

One simple way of doing this is by drawing people's attention (perhaps at the start of a time of singing) to the fact that we worship through Christ, perhaps by reading the following scripture or having everyone read it together: 'Through Jesus, therefore, let us continually offer to God a sacrifice of praise— the fruit of lips that confess his name' (Hebrews 13:15).

Similarly, you can remind people of the image of the curtain in the temple, and how Jesus' death has torn this curtain in two, allowing us to enter into the presence of God. To help them picture it, you can read Hebrews 10:19–22 and perhaps even set up a visual aid of a curtain, which can be torn down or flung back.

Sometimes it is right to remind people of God's holiness. You can read out Hebrews 12:18–29, focusing on the words 'Let us be thankful, and so worship God acceptably with reverence and awe, for our "God is a consuming fire"' (vv. 28–29), perhaps combined with a powerful musical accompaniment or a song that speaks of God's awesome holiness. You might also get creative with fire images: just be careful not to burn the place down!

Most of us will be familiar with singing about Jesus as the sacrificial lamb killed in our place. How often, though, do we sing about or identify Jesus in our worship as our high priest, our mediator, our one and only way to God the Father? One notable example of a song based on this theme is 'Before the throne of God above'.[14] You could use this contemporary setting of an old hymn text and encourage people to reflect on Jesus as the one who intercedes for us in heaven.

You can bring out the trinitarian dynamic of worship by intentionally choosing songs that reflect a balance of the persons of the Trinity. Rather than singing always to 'Lord' or 'Jesus', pick a single hymn[15] or a set of songs that focus in turn on the Father,[16] the Son[17] and the Holy Spirit.[18] Let the language of the Trinity infuse itself into your worship life through your prayers, songs and liturgies. In *Worshipping Trinity*, Robin Parry makes other suggestions for engaging people creatively with the Trinity, including a description of a powerful Trinity dance.

However we approach the concept of the Trinity, the fundamental thing is to remember that Jesus himself leads us into the presence of Father God, by the Spirit. The fact that he chooses to use us as co-leaders, through our voices, song selections, prayers, creative worship activities and leadership gifts, is a privilege and a high calling. The next part of this book will consider more practical ways in which we might play our part in worship leading more fully, with attitudes that are more and more inspired by Jesus.

 WORSHIP EXPERIENCE

Look at your hand. Examine your fingers, the creases, the nails, the dirt. Think about the fact that Jesus had flesh and blood— male hands, not the marble or plaster of a statue. They were probably a bit more worn than yours, perhaps dirtier, but they had skin, bones, nails. Imagine what Jesus' hands might have looked like when he reached out to touch someone, to heal a leper, when he broke bread at the last supper, when he washed the disciples' feet. He had flesh-and-blood hands.

Reflect on this passage:

In bringing many sons and daughters to glory, it was fitting that God, for whom and through whom everything exists, should make the pioneer of their salvation perfect through what he suffered. Both the one who makes people holy and those who are made holy are of the same family. So Jesus is not ashamed to call them brothers and sister. He says, 'I will declare your name to my brothers and sisters; in the assembly I will sing your praises.' ... Since the children have flesh and blood, he too shared in their humanity so that by his death he might break the power of him who holds the power of death—that is, the devil—and free those who all their lives were held in slavery by their fear of death. For surely it is not angels he helps, but Abraham's descendants. For this reason he had to be made like his brothers and sisters in every way, in order that he might become a merciful and faithful high priest in service to God, and that he might make atonement for the sins of the people.

Because he himself suffered when he was tempted, he is able to help those who are being tempted.
HEBREWS 2:10–12, 14–18 (TNIV)

How are you feeling right now? Spend a moment thinking about it. Are you thirsty, happy, tired, exhausted, aching, sleepy? Remember, Jesus has experienced all those feelings, and bigger emotions too—love, loneliness, joy, despair. He calls you his brother or sister; he knows how you feel. Why not spend a moment now, talking to him about it?

✜

PART 2

....

INTRODUCTION

WHY JESUS?

When we set out to explore worship in the Bible, we probably find ourselves turning to the same few passages—the Psalms, the life of David, perhaps an occasional verse in the epistles that mentions singing. If we are feeling really brave, we may take a look at worship in Revelation. Yet there is so much more that the Bible can teach us about worship, if we only know how to go about finding it.

King David is often held up as a worship leading hero because he fits our common stereotype of a worship leader: he writes songs, and he plays something resembling a guitar. We are not denying that there are useful lessons to be learnt from David: all scripture is 'God-breathed' and has something to teach us (2 Timothy 3:16). But isn't Jesus supposed to be our ultimate role model in everything, including how we might approach worship both in our personal lives and when we gather as church? Instead of seeing worship as just singing, writing songs and twanging away at a lump of wood and some wires, we can find in Jesus a living, breathing example of worship in Spirit and in truth.

The second part of this book focuses on the life of Jesus in the Gospel of Luke, and asks what principles we might learn from his life and worship. It then seeks to apply those principles in our own context—broadly speaking, leading gathered worship in Western evangelical/charismatic churches. It aims to take seriously the challenge of leading worship in a Christ-like way, to the glory of God and for the benefit of the local churches where we find ourselves serving.

WHY LUKE?

Have you ever watched a biopic—a film telling the story of a famous or interesting person? If so, you will probably have noticed that its portrayal of the character is usually partial. The film maker has only 90 minutes or a couple of hours, so they choose an angle on that person, a perspective through which to tell the story. Watching *Walk the Line*,[1] the Johnny Cash story, you see the dramatic, controversial angle: his early fame, his addictions and his relationship with June Carter. The film gives you a very different view of the country legend than Steve Turner's biography, *The Man Called Cash*,[2] which looks at the whole of his life through the window of his faith.

Similarly, each of the Gospels has a particular take on the man called Jesus. Writing from different points of view, with different audiences in mind and different storytelling styles, each writer gives us a contrasting angle. It's not that one is more correct than the others; each one complements the others so that, when you step back, you get a fuller picture than one Gospel alone would have provided. At the same time, it is important to get to know each Gospel on its own terms, so that we can see the unique contribution it brings to the revelation of Jesus.

Because of this, we chose to begin our exploration of how Jesus might lead worship by studying just one Gospel: Luke. In one sense, our choice was arbitrary. Luke was simply a Gospel we had always liked and had already spent some time studying. As we have spent longer reflecting on Luke's writings, however, we have found that he brings out unique aspects of Jesus' character, which speak powerfully to our present age.

For example, Luke is keen to emphasize Jesus' concern for the poor, the underdog, women and children.[3] Living, as we do, in an era when evangelical Christians in the West are mindful once again of our role in bringing 'good news to the poor', Luke's Gospel can help us to see how this relates to our worship. As we seek to welcome all kinds of people from our society into church, it is very helpful to see how Luke depicts Jesus as one who always knew how to welcome others with love (see 5:27–32; 7:36–50; 14:1–14).

As the man who also wrote Acts and spent time with Paul on his missionary travels (Acts 20:7), Luke presents an 'orderly account' in his Gospel, based on the eye witnesses to Jesus' life, so that his friend Theophilus may know 'the certainty of the things you have been taught' (Luke 1:1–4). He puts stories and sayings about Jesus together in creative ways to show clearly Jesus' mission to serve and die for others. This has particular relevance for today's self-serving culture.

Luke mentions the Holy Spirit more than any other Gospel writer. In our church worship we can have an uncertain or incomplete grasp of the role of the Spirit, but Luke helps us to see how he relates to Jesus and, by implication, to us and our practice of worship.

We would encourage you to read the following chapters of this book with the text of the Luke's Gospel open, allowing yourself to be challenged by Luke's picture of Jesus to think how you might go about leading worship in your context in a way that more closely reflects his heart and values.

✛

Chapter 2

HUMBLE SERVANT

A friend of ours was doing what is known as 'detached youth work' at a Christian conference, hanging around the youth venue, chatting to the young people who chose not to join in with the organized programme. She fell into conversation with one of them and got around to asking why he didn't go along to the teaching and worship sessions. 'I don't need to,' was his reply. A high-profile Christian leader had prophesied over him that he was going to be a worship leader when he grew up, and he was just waiting around for that to happen.

Our friend was both bemused and concerned. On a number of levels, it was a tragic misunderstanding—to think that because someone has prophesied a powerful ministry in your future, you don't need to develop your discipleship through teaching and fellowship. The young man also seemed to think that a calling as a worship leader meant a full-time position on a big stage, with fame and associated trappings, as if he were a rock star.

'You do realize,' she suggested to him, 'that that prophecy could just as well mean you'll have a fruitful ministry among a few old ladies in some local church for many years?' As the daughter of a worship leader, she knew that 'success' in worship ministry means far more than leading at a big conference or releasing a CD.

We might laugh at this young man and his naive assumptions, but if we search our own hearts and motives, are we really so different? How would we rate a successful ministry in our own lives? Does the worship leaders' pecking order go something like this as far as you are concerned?

1 Big in the US.
2 UK number one worship CD.
3 Leads worship at big conferences.
4 Employed by a church to lead worship.
5 Has some songs published in a worship book.
6 Leads worship in a big church with a great band.
7 Leads in a small church with a struggling music group.
8 Plays in the band.
9 On the rota for the sound desk.
10 Leads the music when everybody else is on holiday...

Be honest, have you ever slotted yourself into an order like this? It is our fallen human nature that considers success to mean fame, power and recognition—precisely the opposite of the humility that we are called to demonstrate (Proverbs 18:12; Matthew 6:5–6; Luke 14:10–11; Philippians 2:3).

How we define 'success' as a worship leader is an essential issue for us, and we should take heart from the knowledge that, throughout his ministry, Jesus had to wrestle with similar matters. 'What does it mean to be Son of God?' and 'What kind of Messiah am I?' were two vital questions for Jesus to resolve, and the first was never posed more clearly than in his battle with the devil in the wilderness after his baptism (Luke 4:1–13).

BAKED GOODS AND OTHER TEMPTATIONS

In Luke's Gospel, Jesus is often portrayed as symbolizing Israel, and here, where his 40 days parallel Israel's 40 years in the wilderness, his tests and temptations are likened to those of Israel in the desert.[1] If you are not convinced, notice that, in answering all three temptations, Jesus quotes from Deuteronomy (8:3; 6:13, 16) passages that relate to Israel's wilderness testing.

In one sense, these temptations were not completely unique to

Jesus. Of course, only he could be tested as the incarnate Son of God, but he was also being tempted as a representative of fallen humankind. His temptations reflect the kind of testing we all go through as God's chosen people, the new Israel—so you and I should be able to relate to them.

Take the first one: 'The devil said to him, "If you are the Son of God, tell this stone to become bread"' (4:3). Now, there's nothing inherently wrong with making or eating bread, so what is the potential sin here? In part, it was a temptation to break the fast to which God had called Jesus, but there was more. Look at how the devil sets it up: '*If* you are the Son of God...' This is a temptation for Jesus to justify himself—his identity, his role. The devil is saying, 'Prove it!' Have you ever had that voice in your head?

'*If* you are the worship leader, make your church worship!'

'*If* you are a songwriter, write some worship hits!'

'*If* you are good at what you do, demand more pay, power and recognition!'

As a female worship leader, Sara has struggled a lot with this temptation, as most role models within the area have been male. She has sometimes got the impression that you're not so 'anointed' if you're not a young man with a guitar. What about a girl with a piano? The temptation is to think, 'I'll prove that I've been called to lead worship too, I'll prove I'm as good as any young-man-with-guitar' every time she steps on to a stage. It's the wrong motivation (even though girls can rock too!).

Sometimes, we can do something that is technically right (like making bread or leading worship in a certain way), but with wrong motivations. We do it to prove ourselves. We can be tempted to justify our position by using God-given gifts for selfish reasons. Theologian Joel Green says of this passage, '[The devil] starts by urging Jesus to use his power in his own way to serve his own ends; he thus reinterprets "Son of God" to mean the opposite of faithful obedience and agency on God's behalf.'[2]

Notice that the devil reinterprets 'Son of God': he defines it in a way contrary to God's will and purpose. How often do we allow ourselves to be tempted to reinterpret 'worship leader' as something that is the opposite of 'faithful obedience and agency on God's behalf'?

The second temptation has an even greater connection with our approach to worship:

The devil led him up to a high place and showed him in an instant all the kingdoms of the world. And he said to him, 'I will give you all their authority and splendour, for it has been given to me, and I can give it to anyone I want to. So if you worship me, it will all be yours.' Jesus answered, 'It is written: "Worship the Lord your God and serve him only"' (vv. 5–8).

It had been prophesied that Jesus would be sovereign over all the nations (see Psalm 2:8 or Luke 1:33). Like the young man in our story earlier, Jesus was destined by God to be 'successful'. So why should he not just go for that success straight away?

Jesus knew that the path to the fulfilment of his calling was not the easy route but the hard way. He was not going to take the nations by force, by superior firepower. He was called to walk the path of humility, of service, of self-sacrifice. His road led not to a palace with a throne but a hill with a cross.

Jesus knew, too, that if he went along any other route, he would be taking the glory away from God. 'Worshipping the devil' is easier than we might think: you don't have to sacrifice virgins or play heavy metal records backwards. Any form of idolatry, putting anything— your instrument, your ministry, money, even your family (Luke 14:26)—before God is a way of worshipping the one who tempts you to do so. The Israelites in the wilderness were amazingly quick to forget God and worship idols (Exodus 32:1–6) and, often, so are we. Yet Jesus knew that there is only one who deserves our worship. He refused to achieve 'success' in his ministry by taking the easy road offered to him by the devil, because he knew that this was a form of idolatry.

Have there been times when you have found yourself on a 'high place'—perhaps at the end of a worship time that has gone really well? Or when a song you've written has been chosen for some special use? At these times, have you envisaged a future full of glory for yourself, in which you can be famous, powerful and adored, if only you will choose to pursue that vision above God's will? How do you deal with that?

The third temptation places Jesus at the highest point of the temple—probably the royal colonnade, which overlooked a deep ravine.[3] The devil has been thwarted by scripture twice, so now he tries his own quotation: '"If you are the Son of God," he said, "throw yourself down from here. For it is written: 'He will command his angels concerning you to guard you carefully; they will lift you up in their hands, so that you will not strike your foot against a stone'"' (Luke 4:9–11).

This is interesting because, in just a few verses' time (v. 29–30), Jesus is saved by God from being thrown over a cliff. Of course, God can be trusted to fulfil his promises to us, but Jesus knew that he was not to test God or his own powers by doing something stupid, with the underlying motive of drawing attention to himself. He replied simply, 'It says: "Do not put the Lord your God to the test"' (v. 12).

Not many of us will be tempted to leap from the roof of St Paul's Cathedral, but we might do something not dissimilar in terms of leading worship. For example, do we ever loudly proclaim that we haven't bothered to plan anything for a worship time, to make ourselves look more spiritual and to 'test' God by expecting him to lead us anyway? Or do we consider taking a 'leap of faith'—perhaps a rash financial decision or relationship choice—which has a veneer of spirituality but is actually all about what we want? Do we loudly expect healing miracles in church services, not out of compassion for the sick but rather because we hope they will bolster our own ego and ministry?

In each of these temptations, Jesus has a choice about the definition of his role as the Son of God. Does the title mean someone powerful, performing crowd-pleasing miracles and ruling over the world by force and might? Each time, Jesus chooses to say, 'No'. Instead, he chooses to define Son of God as one who is obedient, humble and self-sacrificing.

As we define 'worship leader', which path will we choose?

'DON'T TELL ANYONE—I'M THE WORSHIP LEADER'

You are chatting to someone in church before the service starts. They're a newcomer, asking generally about what goes on. Then they casually say, 'You're the worship leader, aren't you?' Immediately you pin them against the wall, eyes wide, casting around to see if anyone else has heard them. 'Yes,' you admit in a whisper, 'I am the worship leader', and you go on to warn them not to tell anyone else. Who knows what might happen if people found out your true identity...?

It sounds crazy, but isn't this exactly what Jesus does in the following passage from Luke's Gospel?

Once when Jesus was praying in private and his disciples were with him, he asked them, 'Who do the crowds say I am?' They replied, 'Some say John the Baptist; others say Elijah; and still others, that one of the prophets of long ago has come back to life.' 'But what about you?' he asked. 'Who do you say I am?' Peter answered, 'The Christ of God.' Jesus strictly warned them not to tell this to anyone (9:18–21).

Where the NIV says 'strictly warned', you could also translate the word as 'commanded' or 'ordered'.[4] In other words, Jesus was laying down the law to his disciples. Once again, the issue was about how Jesus wanted to define the titles given to him. We read words such as 'Messiah' and 'Christ' today—the Hebrew and Greek terms for 'the anointed one'—and think of them in the light of Jesus. We associate them with the Son of God, with his divinity, with his dying on a cross. But for Jesus' contemporaries, their hope in a coming Messiah involved very different preconceptions. The place where they lived was occupied territory, and people were looking out for a political revolutionary, a military deliverer who could conquer the Romans by force.

This was in sharp contrast to Jesus' own definition of Messiah. Once his identity was out in the open, he was forced to redefine it radically for the disciples. If they were expecting a conquering hero-king, they were going to be disappointed. In a stunning piece of expectation management, Jesus turns their idea of Messiah on its head: 'The Son of Man must suffer many things and be rejected by the elders, chief priests and teachers of the law, and he must be killed and on the third day be raised to life' (v. 22).

In Luke's Gospel we don't read Peter's response, 'Never, Lord! This shall never happen to you!' or Jesus' rebuke, 'Get behind me, Satan!' (Matthew 16:22–23). But we can perhaps imagine the disciples' perplexed faces, the sick feeling in their stomachs, their incredulity at what Jesus is suggesting. A suffering Messiah? Rejected by the religious leaders? Killed and then resurrected? Surely Jesus was using metaphorical language again; he could not mean it literally!

PLAYING DEAD

Not only does Jesus redefine the disciples' concept of Messiah, he also goes on to recast their roles as followers of the Messiah. Not just the first disciples but anyone who would follow him (yes, that means us too) has to choose to follow that same road. These men knew what 'taking up your cross' meant (Luke 9:23). Walking behind Jesus was not the road to glory: it could be compared to the moment when an American death-row prisoner leaves his cell for the execution chamber and the guards shout, 'Dead man walking'. As Leon Morris explains, 'When a man from one of their villages took up a cross and went off with a little band of Roman soldiers, he was on a one-way journey. He would not be back. Taking up the cross meant the utmost in self denial.'[5]

We probably didn't count on things getting this heavy when we signed up for the worship band! And yet, in one of his great upside-down statements, Jesus explains that this is not about depressed, self-hating misery, but quite the contrary. Yes, if anyone wants to keep life for themselves, they will lose it; but, Jesus says, if you give up your life for me, you will find true life. THE MESSAGE paraphrases it like this: 'Self-help is no help at all. Self-sacrifice is the way, *my* way, to finding yourself, your true self. What good would it do to get everything you want and lose you, the real you?' (vv. 24–25).

Following Jesus, leading worship like Jesus, must be about self-sacrifice, choosing others before ourselves, letting go of our lives—only to find that as we do so, we discover who we really are, the reason we were created, and the plans and future that God has for us.

Sam was asked by the Jubilate Group to start a new worship songwriters' project, so he gathered a group of grassroots writers. We decided together that all the songs needed to be born in the local church context, but should then be critiqued by the whole group when we met together, and via an online forum. It has been a tough lesson in humility to put our songs (our babies!) out there for others to question the music, the theology and the grammar, and often we have had to die to selfish attitudes in order to serve the church better. But it has also been a great joy, as the improved songs have been recorded and shared as free MP3s and sheet music on www.RESOUNDworship.org. The more we have been able to 'lose ourselves' in the process, the more we have seen God use the songs all over the world. In just twelve months we had over 1800 subscribers and many emails of appreciation. We have been glad that we laid down our original preferences to allow the songs to serve a wider constituency.

What is the implication of 'dying to self' for church worship? It means we ought to consider our motives and actions. Are we quicker to be at the front leading, rather than serving in other ways, such as filing the music, putting out the chairs or tidying up the PA? If a church leader asks us to play a song we don't like so much, or to play in a style that doesn't make us sound as good as we would like, what is our attitude towards them?

If we choose songs for worship, we ought to consider what motivates our decisions. Do we major on our favourites, the songs that make the band or our own voices sound good? Or do we pick the ones that best serve the meeting and the people gathered? Sam once heard someone say, 'If I was in a secular band, I would choose the songs I liked to play, not what my audience wanted to hear. Why can't worship be the same?' The answer is simple: if we follow the lead of Jesus, we must die to our own preferences in order to serve the congregations we lead. A hallmark of those who lead worship with the attitude of Jesus is that they put the needs of others before themselves; it means leading with a servant attitude.

THE PHARISEE AND THE TAX COLLECTOR

How confident are you when you come to worship? More important, in what do you place your confidence? We considered in the previous chapter this amazing truth from Hebrews 10:19: 'We have confidence to enter the Most Holy Place by the blood of Jesus.' Unfortunately, we are inclined to forget that our confidence in entering into worship can come only via the blood of Jesus, never from our own acts of righteousness. That is what the Pharisee needed to hear in these verses from a story Jesus told:

To some who were confident of their own righteousness and looked down on everybody else, Jesus told this parable: 'Two men went up to the temple to pray, one a Pharisee and the other a tax collector. The Pharisee stood up and prayed about himself: "God, I thank you that I am not like other men—robbers, evildoers, adulterers—or even like this tax collector. I fast twice a week and give a tenth of all I get"' (Luke 18:9–12).

We might not see it immediately, but this Pharisee was actually going beyond what was expected of him in the law. Fasting was commanded once a year, on the Day of Atonement (Leviticus 16:29), not twice a week, as many Pharisees did it. The law asked for a tithe of all crops (Deuteronomy 14:22), but Jesus tells us that Pharisees even tithed their garden herbs (Luke 11:42). The man in the story is making a huge show of his righteousness rather than considering how he might be guilty of a deeper sin—pride.

Does our worship ever get a bit like this? Do we sometimes think of our efforts, the time we spend in prayer or worship, the things we do for others, the soundness of our theology, as a means of earning our place in God's kingdom? Or, at least, do we believe that they set us above others whom we judge as somehow inferior: robbers/evildoers/adulterers/other members of the music group...

Compare this to the attitude of the tax collector. Remember that tax collectors at the time were considered to be collaborators with the occupying Roman army, collecting taxes for them and creaming off the top whatever excess they liked. They were despised, seen as worse than scum. But this tax collector knows his place before God: '[He] stood at a distance. He would not even look up to heaven, but beat his breast and said, "God, have mercy on me, a sinner"' (Luke 18:13).

In a physical position of utter humility (sometimes, being on our knees or even our faces before God is exactly where we need to be), the tax collector does not place his confidence in his own achievements, his acts of worship or his service, but throws himself upon the mercy of God. Jesus goes on to shock his audience, turning their expectations upside down by saying, 'I tell you that this man, rather than the other, went home justified before God. For all those who exalt themselves will be humbled, and those who humble themselves will be exalted' (v. 14).

There comes a point in our worship (and maybe it is the starting point) where we need to assume this kind of position before God—the position of humility, recognizing our unworthiness, acknowledging that all our good works, all our preparation and rehearsal, all our adherence to laws and rules, or even going beyond them, means *nothing*. As Paul says (and he had been a Pharisee himself), all of our self-righteousness is rubbish compared to Christ's righteousness (Philippians 3:8–9). *The Message* translates these verses particularly vividly:

Compared to the high privilege of knowing Christ Jesus as my Master, firsthand, everything I once thought I had going for me is insignificant—dog dung. I've dumped it all in the trash so that I could embrace Christ and be embraced by him. I didn't want some petty, inferior brand of righteousness that comes from keeping a list of rules when I could get the robust kind that comes from trusting Christ—God's righteousness.

We need to come to worship humbly. We need to come in repentance for our sin. Is there any time for that in your church services? Is there any period where people can say, 'Lord, have mercy on me?' Below are some ways you could do this in a group setting, but before you lead others, the following 'Worship experience' will give you space to say 'Lord, have mercy' for yourself.

 WORSHIP EXPERIENCE

The Jesus Prayer is an ancient treasure of the Eastern Orthodox Church, a very simple, repeated plea based on three passages from Luke's Gospel (17:13; 18:13, 38): 'Lord Jesus Christ, Son of God, have mercy on me, a sinner.'

If you can, find a quiet place without distractions. You may wish to light a candle, look at an icon of Christ or focus on a picture of a calm nature scene, to keep your eyes from wandering. Then slowly breathe in, quietly saying the first half of the prayer, and breathe out as you say the second part.

Unlike meditation in some other religions, the goal is not to empty your mind but to fill it with nothing but Jesus. The prayer acknowledges our need for forgiveness and repentance, while proclaiming who Jesus is. Repeat the prayer as many times as you like (some Orthodox monks say it hundreds of times per day) and allow God to make himself known to you in the quiet of your heart.

 WORSHIP IDEAS

In a church or small group setting, there are three important parts to any time of confession: the opportunity to reflect on personal sin, the opportunity to confess that sin, and a proclamation that sin is forgiven in Christ. This final section is sometimes called Absolution and, in some traditions, only ordained clergy are allowed to pronounce it. If you think that might be the case in your church, it is worth checking with a leader.

Traditional liturgical prayers offer one way of confessing sin and can have great value for many people. Others will find more imaginative, multi-sensory approaches to confession helpful. Here are some creative suggestions for helping people grasp what forgiveness means.

- Write sins down on paper, then nail the paper to a simple wooden cross. The sound of hammer and nails echoing through a church hall can be spine-tingling. Absolution could be brought through pieces of paper printed with a verse such as Psalm 103:12 or 1 John 1:9, which people could take away with them.
- Reflect on sin by holding a dirt-covered stone in your hands, then place it in a bucket of water to wash it. Somebody could read out Psalm 51 (or have it printed for people to read) as

this happens. Take the clean stone away as a reminder of forgiveness.

- Write a confession on 'flash paper', then put it in a metal tin and drop a match on it. The paper immediately burns up, safely and without smoke.

- Watch the crucifixion scene from a film of Jesus' life, or a series of still images of the cross, using *Agnus Dei* by Rufus Wainwright or the *Agnus Dei* to the tune of Barber's *Adagio* by All Angels, as a soundtrack.[6] Afterwards, have a time of silence for people to confess their sin, before saying the following prayer together (based on John 1:29): 'Jesus, the Lamb of God, who takes away the sins of the world, washes you clean of all sin.'

You could also use a song expressing the ancient prayer *Kyrie eleison* (Greek for 'Lord, have mercy'—for example, Andy Piercy's 'Father, hear our prayer'[7]). Our favourite setting of the text is by Dinah Reindorf from Ghana and can be found in the book *Sing Glory*.[8]

PETER GETS IT RIGHT

Jesus' disciples can be a great comfort to us: they sometimes get things right, but often they mess up spectacularly. We can certainly relate to that in our experience of worship leading.

Let's start with the disciples getting it right: take a look at Luke 5:1–11. Peter is more than happy to let Jesus use his boat as an impromptu stage for a spot of lakeside preaching. Then, once the teaching is over (or, at least, the spoken part of it), Jesus asks something more unusual of him. Jesus gets involved with the disciples' passion, their craft, and encourages them to take a step of faith with him. He invites them to push the boat out (both literally and metaphorically), to see faith in action by trying for one last catch of fish.

Of course, Peter might respond with pride and unbelief: 'I'm the fisherman here; we've been fishing all night. What would a carpenter or rabbi know about it?' But he doesn't. In humility, he trusts and obeys Jesus. And when we do that, like Peter, we begin to see miraculous things happen. In his case, it's a catch of fish so big that the boat begins to sink.

Once again, Peter's response is the right one. Like the prophet Isaiah many years before (see Isaiah 6:1–8), he falls to his knees in the presence of such holiness and power, saying, 'Go away from me, Lord; I am a sinful man!' (Luke 5:8). He knows that he is totally unworthy to be with Jesus, to be used by him in such a way.

Have you ever reached a moment like that? Do we come to worship with that kind of attitude—that we are unworthy, sinful, on our knees? We have already discussed some worship ideas that might help a congregation to reach that point. If we do lead people down this path, however, we must also make sure we move on to the next step in the story: the proclamation of our worthiness, not in our own efforts but in Jesus' decision to make us so. Like the angel touching Isaiah's lips with the coal (Isaiah 6:6–7), Jesus reassures Peter that he need not be afraid, that he has chosen him as one who will be 'catch men and women' (Luke 5:10). It is vital that we do the same when people recognize their own sin and unworthiness; it is then our role to proclaim the truth that in Christ they are made worthy. The gospel does contain some bad news (that we are all sinners, unable to save ourselves) but we should always leave people with the overriding good news—that Jesus loves them and makes them clean and justified to stand in his presence.

The disciples mess up

The disciples start with the right attitude but it is not long before their motives sour (Luke 9:46–55). They have some success in ministry when Jesus sends them out, at the beginning of Luke 9, and it seems that this success sows pride in their hearts. Despite the fact that Jesus restates his commitment to the road of self sacrifice in verse 44, Luke records three self-centred episodes from the disciples in a row: 'An argument started among the disciples as to which of them would be the greatest' (v. 46).

The image of grown men bickering over who is the greatest seems rather comical, and yet, if we are honest, we have probably had similar conversations. For instance, when speaking to other church leaders, do we drop in comments about how many people have been attending our services recently—just so that they know? Or do we casually mention the name of some famous worship leader we have met? Worse, do we spiritualize our boasting: 'God has blessed us with some great worship times recently'?

The disciples' sin here is pride; in the kingdom of God, there is no ranking in terms of status. Jesus explains that those who consider themselves least are 'great' (not 'greatest' in the Greek[9]) in the kingdom of heaven (v. 48b). To illustrate his point, he brings out a little child. In our day and age, children have an elevated status. Many parents almost idolize their little ones, and society recognizes their rights and dignity. In Jesus' time, however, children were considered some of the least of all: they were weak, dependent and unimportant. Yet Jesus said that if the disciples welcomed these lowly ones, they welcomed not only him but also the one who sent him, God the Father (v. 48a).

We need to think through the implications of this teaching for the way we lead worship. Are there people we neglect to 'welcome' in our worship services? How much do you think about the needs of children,[10] or those who are very old? Are people with special needs included in our worship?[11] Perhaps even more pressing is the consideration of those who are not yet Christian: are your worship practices and language accessible for visitors and seekers? Jesus would challenge us to welcome the minorities and include them—to make the 'least' actually the most important.

It is clear from our passage in Luke that this notion is fairly alien to the disciples, and John tries to clarify the position, thereby scoring the second own goal of the day: '"Master," said John, "we saw a man driving out demons in your name and we tried to stop him, because he is not one of us"' (v. 49).

John thinks that they, as the disciples who travel around with Jesus, have cornered the market on using Jesus' name. Essentially, their sin here is selfishness, wanting to keep Jesus for themselves and denying access to him for others.

To what extent do we do this? Think about churches or groups that worship differently from the way you think is 'correct'. Are you tempted to bad-mouth them in front of others? Do you resent their success? Sometimes we might even doubt that they can really connect with God, because they are not part of our 'holy club'. Now, we are right to test theology and practice against the truth of scripture; it is not wrong to engage our critical faculties. But Luke shows that we should be careful about passing judgment over other people's ministries, and especially cautious about how we communicate that judgment to others.

The disciples' third mistake is simply laughable. James and John (nicknamed 'Sons of Thunder' by Jesus in Mark 3:17) decide that some Samaritans should be punished for not welcoming Jesus. They may have been remembering 2 Kings 1:10–12, an eye-watering passage of scripture where Elijah calls down fire from heaven upon two captains and their 50 men, because the king had been consulting other gods. So the Sons of Thunder storm up to Jesus to say, 'Lord, do you want us to call fire down from heaven to destroy them?' (Luke 9:54).

This seems like quite an overreaction on their part, and it's a response that goes completely against the heart of Jesus. Once again, they have failed to grasp the sort of Messiah Jesus is—not a bullying military ruler taking the world by force, but a humble servant.

How do you respond to people who are rude to you, those who criticize your playing or your song choices? What about church members who reject your worship style or your point of view? Do people ever get a 'fiery thunderbolt' of words from you, or a burning look or a ticking time-bomb of passive aggression?

The disciples never quite grasped Jesus' true nature during his earthly life. They just could not understand the upside-down nature of his kingdom. Remarkably, even at the last supper, Luke records another argument about who is the greatest. Jesus' response is brought out particularly well in THE MESSAGE:

'Kings like to throw their weight around and people in authority like to give themselves fancy titles. It's not going to be that way with you. Let the senior among you become like the junior; let the leader act the part of the servant. Who would you rather be: the one who eats the dinner or the one who serves the dinner? You'd rather eat and be served, right? But I've taken my place among you as the one who serves' (Luke 22:25–27).

We know from John's Gospel that Jesus then demonstrated his point by getting down on his hands and knees to do the most menial act of service: washing his disciples' feet (John 13:1–17). And even that act of humble service was not as great as his final one, when he submitted himself to death on a cross, for their sins and for ours.

It is the combination of Jesus' death and resurrection with the coming of the Holy Spirit—to illuminate and enable the disciples—that helps them finally grasp Jesus' kingdom principles. By his blood and his Spirit, the disciples are transformed into humble, serving people, who have the power to heal (Acts 3:6), the compassion to provide for the needy (4:34) and the acceptance to release others into ministry and service (6:3).

We may feel like failures when it comes to having humility in our lives and ministries. But we should take heart that, just as the disciples could be changed by encountering the crucified Jesus and the empowering touch of his Spirit, so can we. As Michael Wilcock puts it, 'When we have admitted how little we, like the disciples, have really grasped about him and about ourselves, we shall appreciate all the more his forbearance and love in giving us repeated opportunities for learning more of his Word, and making the fullest use of what he gives.'[12]

AT LEAST CARE FOR THE LEAST!

In Luke's Gospel Jesus begins his ministry with a powerful manifesto statement, about who he is and what he has come to achieve.

He went to Nazareth, where he had been brought up, and on the Sabbath day he went into the synagogue, as was his custom. And he stood up to read. The scroll of the prophet Isaiah was handed to him. Unrolling it, he found the place where it is written: 'The Spirit of the Lord is on me, because he has anointed me to preach good news to the poor. He has sent me to proclaim freedom for the prisoners and recovery of sight for the blind, to release the oppressed, to proclaim the year of the Lord's favour' (Luke 4:16–19).

'He's so anointed.' We may have heard that phrase used in church settings to imply that someone is specially gifted, has a kind of hotline to God, perhaps in relation to the way they lead worship. Yet here we see Jesus applying it to himself, not in the context of church leadership but to show that he is set apart to serve and transform the lives of the poor, the marginalized and the outcast. Here the empowering of the Spirit is not for an individualized experience, but for the sake of others, for the sake of the least.

It is most likely that synagogues had a kind of lectionary to dictate which passage from the Pentateuch (the first five books of the Old Testament) would be read when the community gathered for prayer, but the reading from the Prophets was chosen by the reader.[13] Jesus must have selected this passage from Isaiah 61 very deliberately, and must have intentionally left out the words about God's vengeance (see Isaiah 61:2b). His ministry had already begun and good reports are already circulating, but in his home town he finds it necessary to be very specific about the kind of calling he is fulfilling.

This shows that Jesus' life of perfect worship to the Father is not only to do with spiritual matters. It is not only about blessing Israel or the important people in society. It is a mission of words and action, proclamation and demonstration. He preaches and lives out good news to the poor, the sick, the lonely. In fact, much of Luke's Gospel is intent on demonstrating Jesus' bias towards the unlovable.[14] In the rush to improve our sung worship, our corporate services, have we missed our calling to worship God by serving the least?

Our previous church felt a challenge to make a difference for our local community in acts of service and blessing. We talked about doing something on a Saturday or a week night, but agreed that people were already very busy and we wouldn't be able to guarantee as good a turn-out as we wanted. So we set aside a whole Sunday (we knew most people would be available as they would normally be at church) and planned projects like renovating a single mum's council flat, redecorating a local school and painting a run-down community hall. But we were very careful in our wording when promoting the events. We did not say, 'Next week we are cancelling the services to do some acts of kindness.' Instead we announced, 'Next week we are taking our worship outside the walls of this building and glorifying God through serving others.' Painting, cleaning and other activities were transformed from mundane tasks into acts of worship. We took seriously the challenge of Colossians 3:23–24: 'Whatever you do, work at it with all your heart, as working for the Lord, not for human masters, since you know that you will receive an inheritance from the Lord as a reward. It is the Lord Christ you are serving.'

It is very encouraging to see events in recent years, such as Hope 08 and Soul in the City, taking seriously the challenge to bless our communities, to serve the least and to bring about what American church leader Rick Warren has called a 'reformation, not of creeds but of deeds',[15] showing the love of God in practical action rather than mere words lobbed from behind the safety of church walls.

The worship team of a church should be leading the way when a congregation decides to bless its community or address a global justice issue, rather than waiting around until the church has 'got over' its social action urge and come back to 'worship'. As worship leaders, we should be on the front line of any such attempts to serve as a church. We should also consider our everyday personal lives—the people we pass in the street, our colleagues at work, our consumer choices and financial gifts. Otherwise, at what point does our music become just noise to God, clashing with our lack of concern and action for justice, the poor and the lonely?

The prophet Amos warns us that God may say, 'Away with the noise of your songs! I will not listen to the music of your harps. But let justice roll on like a river, righteousness like a never-failing stream!' (Amos 5:23–24).

Andy Flannagan has suggested a provocative contemporary paraphrase for these verses:

'I hate your festivals. I cannot stand your worship events. Even though there are thousands of people, and the PA could cause an earthquake, I will not accept them. Even though the band is fantastic, and you have the best worship leader in the world, I have no regard for them. Do you think I care who sells most CDs? Do you think I care what the cool new song is? Away with this individualized, feel-good soundtrack of iPOD "worship". I'm listening to another channel. It's called Justice and Righteousness, and its arriving on a broadband connection that is wider than you can ever imagine. That's what I want to hear. I know when someone's playing MY song.'[16]

This should shock us out of our comfortable, inward-looking worship times and stir us to consider how we might sing the songs of justice that are on God's heart, and live the lives of worship that will bless the least in Jesus' name.

ENGAGING WITH JUSTICE IN SERVICES

If we think about the services we help to lead, how many are 'good news to the poor'? It seems clear from scripture that both worship leaders and those with other creative gifts should be playing their part in corporate worship to communicate and engage worshippers with issues that are on God's heart. In Sunday worship, there are three dimensions: the vertical (to God), the horizontal (towards each other) and a third dimension of engagement with the wider world, through intercession, lament and challenge. It may be that we are least well equipped to worship in the light of that third dimension—a realm with which Jesus seemed to have no problem engaging.

In 2006, someone in our church suggested that we should put on an event to mark the 200th anniversary of the abolition of the slave trade, 25 March 2007. As the church was just around the corner from where Wilberforce and the Clapham Sect based their historic struggle for equality, it seemed like a great opportunity to engage with the issues, so we began some research.

What we did not know when we began was the depth of emotion that the issues would bring up: the injustice of the trade, the scandalous actions of Christians in supporting the barbarism and the tragic fact that slavery and trafficking affect more people than ever today. Yet closest to home was the realization, as we talked to black church members, that prejudice and segregation are still very real issues for many people, even in churches. Our attempts to partner with a local Black Majority church were at first very difficult, as we crashed in with our ideas, blind to the pain of their experiences.

It was humbling to stop, to listen to others, to face up to our failings and try to make the project a living model of unity, equality and reconciliation. In the end, our thoughts gave birth to a number of events: a full-length show called *Sugar Don't Taste So Sweet*, featuring a mix of drama, video and live music; a shorter show taken into local schools; and finally—on the night of the anniversary—a Freedom Day service, where we were able to work together properly with our friends in the Black Majority church. For us, the whole project was a hugely challenging but eye-opening example of how a church's worship and creative team could engage with a social issue.[17]

 WORSHIP IDEAS

We hope that this has got you thinking about how you can engage with similar issues in your church, in ways relevant to you. Here are some other suggestions for engaging congregations in 'third dimension' worship.

- Use a collection of images and statistics from world news or charity websites on a PowerPoint presentation or OHP slide.[18] Use a soundtrack like *The Way You Dream* by 1 Giant Leap for a 'world' feel, or *Dragonfly* by Goldie for something more urban.[19] Encourage people to pray silently for situations as they see them on the screen.
- Set up a prayer station with one or more heavy rucksacks, depending on the size of your event. Print out or write large Galatians 6:2, 'Carry each other's burdens, and in this way you will fulfil the law of Christ.' Instruct people to lift the rucksack and, as they do so, to remember and pray for those (locally or globally) who carry heavy burdens of responsibility, debt, fear and so on. Then, as they take the backpack off, encourage them to consider the freedom they feel, and provide the verses from Matthew 11:28–30 in which Jesus offers rest for the burdened.
- Make use of resources from Tearfund, Christian Aid[20] and other charities with which your church is connected. Often their videos or service resources can highlight areas of poverty or need in the world. Give space for prayer and response.

- Incorporate issues of poverty and justice into your sung worship on a regular basis, not just once or twice a year. Make use of the many songs by the Iona Community (such as 'A touching place'[21]), Andy Flannagan ('Bring heaven to earth'[22]), Tim Hughes ('God of justice'[23]) and Geraldine Latty ('Shout the news'[24]), or write your own.

As our churches seek to look outwards at our communities and the needs of the whole world, let us, as leaders of worship, ensure that our times of worship are not only inward-looking but also reflect the heart of God for a hurting world.

❖

Chapter 3

LEADER WITH AUTHORITY

WHO CARES ABOUT LEADERSHIP?

Jesus once told a story about a rich man who made one of his slaves a leader in charge over the others, to look after them, providing food and care (Luke 12:42–48). If the servant was faithful, he would be rewarded by being given even more authority, over all the rich man's possessions.

'But suppose the servant says to himself, "My master is taking a long time in coming," and he then begins to beat the other servants, both men and women, and to eat and drink and get drunk. The master of that servant will come on a day when he does not expect him and at an hour he is not aware of. He will cut him to pieces and assign him a place with the unbelievers' (vv. 45–46).

Fancy being cut to pieces? No, we don't, either...

If you lead worship in your church, you are a church leader, whether you like it or not. You influence people in the church. Your song choices inform people's theology and voice their praise. Your example is followed by others, both on and off stage.

Jesus takes leadership very seriously and has some harsh words for those who misuse the leadership and authority they have been given. In Luke 11:37–54 he criticizes the religious leaders of the day, listing six 'woes'—ways in which they miss the point, mislead the people and turn the judgment of God upon themselves. Jesus has no hesitation in naming their sin for what it is, and in the process he makes enemies of them, despite the resulting danger to himself.

The good news is that because Jesus takes leadership so seriously, he models for us how it should be done and empowers us to do the same. Like the servant in the story, he will often begin by giving us a small amount of responsibility. Then, as we prove ourselves faithful in it, our spheres of influence increase. Jesus makes the following statement in relation to money, but it can just as easily be applied to leadership: 'Whoever can be trusted with very little can also be trusted with much' (Luke 16:10).

When we think about our attitude towards leadership, are we intentionally working to be faithful in what Jesus gives us and mature into our leadership roles and responsibilities?[1] Have we considered the effectiveness of how we lead our band or our worship team, and our faithfulness in leading congregations? Before we focus on these important issues in detail, we should begin by looking at how we 'lead' (or take responsibility for) our own lives.

DITCHES, PLANKS AND OTHER LEADERSHIP HAZARDS

Luke 6 gives us various teachings from Jesus, delivered from 'a level place' (v. 17). He is in good form when we get to verses 39–42; he has probably been speaking for a while and now he's in full flow. There is the comical (if not very politically correct) image of one blind man leading another blind man, and both of them ending up in a ditch. Then there's the one about the fellow with a huge plank lodged in his eye, starting to prod around in some other poor man's face, who only has a speck to deal with.

The stories are laughable, but perhaps less funny if you are the blind man trying to lead, or the man with a plank in his eye, whom Jesus calls a 'hypocrite'. Even worse is the situation of those who have to follow these failing leaders, as they are dragged into ditches and wrongly accused. Jesus continues this passage by speaking about trees with bad roots that don't bear fruit (vv. 43–45), and houses built on shaky foundations (vv. 46–49). The point he is making again and again is 'get yourself right before you begin to lead others'. Tree roots and foundations are unseen, yet they have a huge impact on the fruit or the stability of the ministry that rests on them.

What is unseen in your life? Are there attitudes of anger, resentment or bitterness towards other people bubbling under the surface, which need dealing with? How about your financial dealings: do you honour God with your money? How do you treat your family when the doors are closed? Do they get the best of your love and attention, or the dregs at the end of the day? Is your sexual life following God's best path or are there secret lusts that need to be worked through in confession, and steps that need taking towards wholeness?

These questions are not meant to be guilt-inducing but are intended to help us honestly assess our 'secret' life, the things that people don't see but have a lasting impact on our leadership and ministry. We need to experience not a worldly sorrow and guilt over our sin, but what Paul calls 'godly sorrow', which 'brings repentance that leads to salvation and leaves no regret' (2 Corinthians 7:10). If we are 'blind' to problem areas in our lives, we may find ourselves, and those we lead, in a ditch. Or we may spend our time pointing the finger at other people's faults without realizing that our own sins are beginning to cover our faces.

We all need to have a small group of people with whom we can have honest conversations about such issues. We need to be intentional about making accountability relationships with appropriate people, people who can ask us hard questions and with whom we can be honest about our failings. None of us is perfect, we all fail, and yet God in his grace provides not only forgiveness and cleansing from our sin by the blood of Jesus on the cross, but also brothers and sisters with whom we can work through our problems and, with their help, know God's victory over sin.

JESUS AND THE NOTION OF AUTHORITY

For some people, the word 'authority' has very negative connotations. It may remind them of an overbearing parent or an abusive teacher, or fear of the police or other government institutions. In our society, we don't generally like to think of ourselves as under anyone's control; we would rather be convinced than coerced. So when we lead worship, do we consider ourselves to be under authority or to hold any position of authority ourselves? Or does the very word send us running for the hills?

Luke's Gospel shows Jesus as one who was described as both coming under and holding authority. In Luke 4:32 and 36, we read that people were amazed by Jesus' authoritative teaching. In Matthew 7:28–29 and Mark 1:22 we learn the same fact, but with the added explanation that he did not teach '…as the teachers of the law'. It wasn't common for rabbis of Jesus' time to teach anything new or original; rather, they offered a mixture of quotes and references. In contrast to them, Jesus spoke as one whose words had authority, without human justification.

Luke also records how Jesus commanded a demon to come out of a man, and the people responded: 'What is this teaching? With *authority* and power he gives orders to evil spirits and they come out!' (4:36, our emphasis).

Jesus' authority was not limited to words or to this world. He also exercised authority in the spiritual realm, a level of reality beyond what we can normally see but which Luke describes as being very real, having an impact on everyday life. Jesus also describes himself as having authority to forgive sin (5:21–26) and acts with authority to drive the merchants out of the temple (19:45–46).

When Jesus is asked by the priests and religious teachers where his authority comes from to do such a radical thing, however, he deftly avoids having to answer the question (20:1–8). At the last supper, he appears to criticize those who exercise authority: 'Jesus said to them, "The kings of the Gentiles lord it over them; and those who exercise authority over them call themselves Benefactors. But you are not to be like that"' (22:25–26).

So how are we to understand this concept of authority, and what relevance does it have for us today, especially if we are involved in leading worship? The key may lie in one of Jesus' encounters with a Gentile centurion.

Someone who understands it

The centurion in Luke 7:1–10 is not a Jew but he is well loved by the Jews for building them a synagogue, so the Jewish leaders take a message from him to Jesus, asking him to come and heal the centurion's sick servant. As Jesus is on his way, a second group of the centurion's friends turn up with a rather strange message:

'Lord, don't trouble yourself, for I do not deserve to have you come under my roof. That is why I did not even consider myself worthy to come to you. But say the word, and my servant will be healed. For I myself am a man under authority, with soldiers under me. I tell this one, "Go," and he goes; and that one, "Come," and he comes. I say to my servant, "Do this," and he does it' (vv. 6–8).

At this point, something happens that never happens at any other point in the Gospels: Jesus *marvels* at someone.[2] He is amazed, blown away. Far from thinking that it is a stupid idea, he praises the centurion for his great faith—greater than he has found in all Israel (v. 9).

The centurion understands the nature of Jesus' authority. He himself is under the authority of his higher-ranking commanders and he has people under his authority. He knows that, in the spiritual realm, Jesus is under the authority of God the Father and has authority over lesser spiritual beings—angels, demons and so on. He knows that you cannot have one without the other: you must be under authority to be able to exercise authority over someone else.

Jesus himself confirms this understanding in Luke 10:17–22. At this point, Jesus is 'full of joy' (v. 21) because the disciples have come back and reported that demons obeyed them in Jesus' name. He explains to them that 'my Father has given me authority over everything' (v. 22, NLT), and that he has passed this authority on to them so that they can have power over the enemy. He is both under the authority of the Father and able to delegate authority to those under him.

It is important to realize that this kind of authority is not a dictatorial, manipulative authoritarianism. Right here in this passage, Jesus uses the Greek word corresponding to the Aramaic *Abba*, the childlike name similar to our 'Daddy', an intimate term of loving devotion used uniquely at this time by Jesus to address the Father.[3] Human sinfulness has twisted 'authority' into a selfish and damaging concept but, at its heart, true authority reflects the perfect relationships of the Trinity: the Father being served by the Son and the Spirit in reciprocal, mutual love.

It is vital to understand this in relation to the way we lead worship. If Jesus himself was both under authority and exercised it over people and the spiritual realm, so must we. We cannot expect to have authority unless we submit ourselves to it, and yet we also cannot think of ourselves as leaders of worship without considering the authority and responsibility we have been given over others.

Firstly and most importantly, we are under the authority of God. As Jesus passed authority on to his disciples to heal the sick, cast out demons (Luke 9:1) and take the message of repentance to all the nations (24:47), so he also passes it on to us. As followers of Christ, we are under the authority of God and he gives us authority in the spiritual and earthly realms to do his will. If God has called you to lead or be involved in worship, in whatever context or medium, he has given you the authority to do so. We do not need to prove ourselves or invent any other earthly credentials. That is why Jesus avoided the priests' questions in 20:1–8: they would not have accepted that his authority came from the Father.

We are under the authority of God, therefore, and yet God has also set up the earthly structures of authority to be a protection and a blessing to us. Paul says to the Romans:

Let everyone be subject to the governing authorities, for there is no authority except that which God has established. The authorities that exist have been established by God. Consequently, whoever rebels against the authority is rebelling against what God has instituted, and those who do so will bring judgment on themselves (Romans 13:1–2).

The writer to the Hebrews also tells us, 'Have confidence in your leaders and submit to their authority, because they keep watch over you as those who must give an account. Do this so that their work will be a joy, not a burden, for that would be of no benefit to you' (Hebrews 13:17, TNIV).

This means that, in a church context, we are to submit (another Bible word that is often unpopular) to those who lead us: ministers, vicars, elders, churchwardens, paid church staff—whatever kind of authority structure is set up. Sometimes we might disagree with them, and it is not wrong to question or discuss, so long as we do it with the right attitude of humility and grace. However, at the end of the day, we are to respect their position as given by God and trust that God will hold them to account for their responsibilities.

In our experience, as we have honoured our leadership in listening to their advice and instruction, it has been very releasing. It is a great safety net to be able to exchange meaningful looks or a few words with our vicars and service leaders while we have been leading worship. On a bigger scale, there was a time when Sam was asked to play at a national conference and, as usual, he took the idea to our vicar. To Sam's surprise, the vicar's reply was 'No', because of things going on in our church at the time and some concerns over the nature of the conference. Sam had to choose whether to accept this decision graciously or complain and grumble over it. He was glad he chose the former, because an opportunity for some week-long training came up around the same time, which he would not have been able to attend if he had led at the conference. God honours us when we honour our leaders.

In very practical terms, think about your relationship with your leaders. Do you act positively within the opportunities they give you to lead or be involved? Do you make a habit of contacting the service leaders or preacher to find out the theme for the service, and try to accommodate it in your planning? Do you lead in a way that honours the wishes of your leaders, or do you sometimes try to push the boundaries so that you can do things your way?

It is easy to feel that once we are behind a microphone we have power. Yet that power must be submitted first to God and second to the leaders who are appointed over us. Only then comes the right to exercise the authority we have over others, with the added responsibility of leading well.

 WORSHIP EXPERIENCE

God is gracious in providing people in authority over us, to lead and inspire us. Spend a moment thinking about this and listening to God. Who are the people that God has sent into your life for this purpose? They could be people in the past or at the present time.

Give thanks to God for these people, mentioning them by name before him and asking him to bless them.

Write a postcard to one of the people, thanking them for taking leadership seriously, and naming some specific things about their ministry that have blessed you. (If you're going to do it, do it now, before you forget!)

JESUS THE LEADER

'Shoegazing' was a style of indie music in the late 1980s. Typified by bands like The Cocteau Twins and The Jesus and Mary Chain, the musicians would stand almost motionless on stage, staring intently at their feet or their guitar effects pedals, lost in a wave of electric guitar noise. While such waves of noise are not notably part of contemporary Christian worship (apart from the odd bit of unintentional feedback), the 'shoegazer' pose is fairly common. Sometimes, with their eyes closed and their head down (or occasionally up towards the ceiling), some worship leaders seem hardly aware of the congregation at all. We could be forgiven for wondering whether they would prefer it if we all went home and left them alone with the Lord!

This pose is probably a misplaced form of humility, an attempt to deflect attention away from the leaders themselves and on to God. But there is something in the title 'worship leader' that gives us a clue to what we are supposed to be doing: *leading* worship.

The truth is, people like to be led. It can be quite uncomfortable to be led by someone who seems lacking in confidence or self-absorbed. We should remember that church is for corporate worship: we are supposed to be coming to God together, to offer a unified expression of praise, prayer, response and so on.

Jesus was not afraid to give instructions to his disciples: 'Put out into deep water and let down the nets'; 'Tell the people to sit on the ground in groups of fifty'; 'Find the donkey that has never been ridden and bring it here' (see Luke 5:4; 9:14; 19:30). There is a right place and time to instruct a congregation. Nobody wants a worship leader to rival the preacher in speaking time or theological complexity. Nor is our role to order or nag people ('I want to see more hands in the air!') but to explain how people can be involved in the next phase of worship. This could include:

• an invitation to sit, stand, or kneel, or some other physical movement.

- an encouragement for people to sing out their own spontaneous songs or call out short praise prayers.
- reading a piece of scripture that fits the flow of worship, and encouraging people to meditate on it for a moment.
- an instruction to pause and consider the blessings of the past week.
- an invitation to pray for a situation, silently or out loud.
- a reminder of some attribute of God, and the suggestion that people consider this as they sing the next song or listen to an instrumental section.

To some, these suggestions may seem completely obvious, but for those who have been taught simply to sing during worship, they may be a cultural shift.

Sam remembers a worship time when people were really getting lost in worship—singing, arms raised, eyes closed. Yet we had just returned from a church weekend away together, and although he felt that people were focused on God, he had a gut instinct that they were forgetting one another. So, as the band continued playing, he encouraged everyone to open their eyes for a moment, and to look around at those beside them, behind them and in front of them. He asked them to consider that God had called each person uniquely and given them a part to play in our church, and that we belonged together as the body of Christ. Then, as the song continued, he encouraged them to sing with their eyes open, exhorting one another with their songs (Ephesians 5:19). A number of people remarked afterwards how helpful this simple instruction had been.

That particular act of leadership was spontaneous; it simply came to Sam at that moment and he had to discern whether or not to go with it. Spontaneous instruction is not the only kind, however. Often it is much safer and more fruitful to plan beforehand the shape and structure of what you plan to do in a time of worship, and sketch out how you are going to lead the congregation through the experience.

To put it simply, if you are going to lead, you have to know where you are going. Jesus certainly did. In the years of preparation before his ministry began, in his reading of the scriptures and his continued times of prayer with the Father, it was made clear to him that he was sent to proclaim the kingdom in word and deed (Luke 4:18–19), and that his work as the Messiah was to be brought to completion through suffering, death and resurrection (9:22). His dramatic meeting with Moses and Elijah on the mount of transfiguration (vv. 28–36) seems to have clarified things for him further: 'They spoke about his departure, which he was about to bring to fulfilment at Jerusalem' (v. 31).

From this point on, Jesus 'set his face' towards Jerusalem (v. 51, NRSV), knowing that this city was the place where he must complete his mission. When some Pharisees tried to warn him that Herod wanted his blood, he was unshakeable in his resolve: 'He replied, "Go tell that fox, 'I will drive out demons and heal people today and tomorrow, and on the third day I will reach my goal.' In any case, I must keep going today and tomorrow and the next day—for surely no prophet can die outside Jerusalem!"' (13:32–33).

As leaders, it is very important for us to follow Jesus' example in seeking God, reading his word and listening to the people he sends our way in order that we might know direction for our ministry. This applies to the big picture—how we want worship in our context to develop over the next few years, the goals we want to achieve as a team, the values and ethos we want to permeate every act of worship in our church. If we lead a worship team, we should surely take time to work through these issues with our group.

LEADERSHIP AND SERVICE PLANNING

Following Jesus' example of knowing our overall direction also applies to smaller-scale matters, particularly how we go about planning a time of corporate worship. Of course, the Spirit can prompt us to speak or lead on the spur of the moment, as we have already seen, but he can also guide us during preparation a few days or even weeks beforehand.

When we (Sam and Sara) are preparing for a time of corporate worship, we go through something like the process outlined in Appendix 1. This encourages us to think of worship as a journey, leading people through a series of different sections or 'movements' of worship, each with a different but interlinked aim. For some people, their only explicit aim will usually be 'glorifying God', and of course that is very important, but it is not the only aim we can have for our worship.

We know that Jesus, as a devout and observant member of the Jewish community, sang the Psalms, so to some extent the range of worship expression found there should be an indication of what we can hope to express in worship. Here are some suggestions:

- Gathering people (Psalm 95:1–2)
- Praising God (66:1–4)
- Remembering God's deeds in recent and personal experience (40:1–3), and in our corporate life and long ago (78:1–4; 136: 1–26)
- Giving thanks (92:1–4)
- Placing trust in God (25:1–3)
- Recognizing God's holiness and majesty (29:1–11; 93:1–5)
- Coming quietly to hear his voice (95:6–7; 131:1–2)
- Contemplating how nature reveals and glorifies God (19:1–6; 104:1–32)
- Intimate adoration (63:1–8)
- Lament, expressing sorrow over disappointment or tragedy (22: 1–2; 137:1–4)
- Confession and absolution: personal (51:1–17) and corporate (130:1–8)
- Intercession: for justice (58:1–11), for the world (67:1–7) and for ourselves (80:1–3)
- Reflecting on and responding to God's word (119:9–16)

- Remembering what God thinks of us (139:1–18)
- Pronouncing blessing (121:5–8)

This is obviously not an exhaustive list but it shows the many emotions that can be expressed, and the many movements of worship into which we can lead people. Sadly, many of them have been forgotten or neglected by contemporary churches, but it is part of our role as worship leaders to revive them.

Some of these expressions may already happen in your church, but may not fall under the remit of worship leader. For example, the pastor or service leader might always lead the confession, or a rota of people might lead the intercessions. It is still worth considering how you might help resource these movements of worship, perhaps drawing them into the singing time or expressing them in some other creative way. Indeed, we want to encourage you strongly, wherever possible, to plan worship as a team exercise, with the service leader or preacher and/or with other creative people who can come up with different movements and expressions of worship.

We hope that the structure in Appendix 1 might help you think through where you are going in leading a corporate worship time, and why you choose the songs and other forms of worship that you use. It has been our experience that, when people engage with this process, their worship leading begins to have shape and they are able to lead people on a worship journey, drawing them closer to God. Have a go and see for yourself!

DEVELOPING A WORSHIP TEAM

If you have responsibility for worship in your context and you want to see it grow, you will have to build a team. Jesus was, perhaps, the ultimate team builder. Just look at the results: he took a ragbag bunch of misfits and transformed them into the kind of leadership team that would take his message and his movement to the far corners of the earth. He built a team that defended and proclaimed his story in the face of persecution and death threats, founded a church that helped to transform history and is still growing today worldwide. Something about what he did with those disciples worked, and we can learn from it as we think about building teams in our churches.

First, he handpicked his team. We might look for worship team members with obvious gifts in music or the creative arts, and of course such gifts are important, but it seems that Jesus was looking first for character. We have already discussed in Chapter 2 how he tested Peter's character, giving him simple tasks such as asking to use his boat and instructing him to go out for a final catch of fish. Peter responded with generosity, trust and obedience (Luke 5:1–11).

This is very important for us to remember. A great singer, musician or artist may join our church, and we can be very tempted to involve them straight away in upfront worship ministry. Yet what do we know about their character? Are they living a life of integrity? Do they respond well to instruction and critique? Often it is helpful to give potential team members small tasks, to see if they are prepared to help with making the coffee or setting up equipment or filing music. If they are prepared to serve with humility and good humour in the small things, they will most probably be a joy to have in the worship team. If someone wanted to lead worship in our church, we would give them the opportunity to lead in a small prayer meeting or a home group, to see how they acted in this context, and with what attitude they received feedback and constructive criticism.

When Sam first joined our previous church, the team operating the PA system was rather demotivated and unskilled. There was, however, one individual who stood out. Chloe would turn up early before services, double check that all the sound was OK, listen to instructions, and enquire about the shape of the service. She was not the most technical or highly trained operator but she certainly had the best attitude. Early on, Sam realized that she could have a major role to play in the worship life of the church. When she showed an interest in drama, he had no reservations about trusting her to head up a fledgling drama and video team. Her professional yet servant attitude so impressed our church and its leaders that we asked her to take a year out of her career to pursue the development of creative arts as a full-time volunteer, and when that came to an end we employed her as a full-time staff member. Her faithfulness in small things proved that we could trust her in a major role.

Jesus had a wider band of followers but he also chose a smaller circle of disciples in whom he invested more time. He made this key decision in an attitude of prayer: 'One of those days Jesus went out to a mountainside to pray, and spent the night praying to God. When morning came, he called his disciples to him and chose twelve of them, whom he also designated apostles' (Luke 6:12–13).

How much do you value prayer and the creation of space to listen to God when you recruit people to be in your team? In particular, have you identified a smaller circle of key individuals whom you plan to mentor and grow, under God's guidance? Sometimes God will lead us to invest in less obvious people, those without the flashy gifts or experience, who may prove to be among our most fruitful relationships. We probably would not discover such people without first going to God in prayer.

Jesus invested a great amount of time and effort in his key team, the apostles. He spent almost all his time with them, often turning from the crowds to speak just to them (Luke 10:23–24), explaining his teaching in greater depth and allowing them to ask questions. We can certainly learn from this as leaders, as it is always worthwhile to create time to go for a coffee or simply chat with key team members. Sam tried to make it a habit to meet with the newer worship leaders that he was mentoring, 30 to 60 minutes before worship rehearsals, to talk and pray through the song choices and any other issues that might have come up for them.

Jesus began by allowing the disciples to observe him as he ministered (7:11). Modelling good practice is essential for any team leader. 'Do what I say, not what I do' is possibly the most useless maxim in the universe. Make sure the people you are mentoring see you minister and notice the preparation that goes in to make the ministry happen. But don't leave it too long before you let them have a go themselves: only a few chapters into Luke's Gospel, Jesus lets the disciples loose!

The disciples' first mission

'When Jesus had called the Twelve together, he gave them power and authority to drive out all demons and to cure diseases, and he sent them out to preach the kingdom of God and to heal the sick' (Luke 9:1–2).

Luke 9 has some important lessons for us about how to release people into ministry. Jesus entrusts the disciples with the very same mission that he himself has exercised so far: to preach the kingdom and heal the sick. He passes his authority and power on to them. There comes a point when we need to deal with any control issues we may have and let someone else have a go at our ministry.

The truth is, Jesus knew that his mission would fail unless he effectively multiplied himself twelve, 72 and then thousands of times over. Notice Luke's care in placing the note about Herod's growing awareness of all that Jesus has done at this specific point in the story (vv. 7–9). He wants us to see that, although Jesus himself is making waves, it is when he sends out others that people really begin to take notice. This should be an encouragement to us to train, equip and release others in ministry.

Jesus does not make it easy for his disciples: he drops them in the deep end, with instructions that sound almost ridiculous. Don't take a walking stick, or a bag, or food, or money, or an extra coat (v. 3). Was Jesus insane? Did he want them to freeze or starve? More importantly, does he expect us to do the same? Must we tell first-time worship leaders to work without a PA, sheet music or instruments? Should we just drop them in it?

We need to understand the cultural context here. Many travelling teachers would make a good living out of walking (with their recognizable wooden stick) from place to place, collecting money in their bag in return for dispensing some 'wisdom'.[4] Often they would begin by staying in one of the more modest houses in the village. Then, if what they said pleased people, they would be invited to better and better houses, trading up as their stay went on.[5]

Jesus is determined that the disciples will bear as little resemblance to these religious salesmen as possible. The gospel is not to be hawked for monetary gain. The disciples are not to trade up, but to honour the lowly houses whose residents first invite them in. Jesus is showing them how to conduct themselves with values that are different from those of the world around them. We should do the same with our teams, ensuring that the glory of God and the serving of the congregation are their highest goal—not money, or recognition, or any other self-centred aim.

The second reason for these instructions is that the disciples are to do as Jesus has done, trusting God, not earthly possessions, for their provision and care. It is tempting to think that if we just had a slightly better guitar or a bigger PA or a bigger team, then our worship would really take off. God does provide these resources for us, and they are not inherently wrong, yet sometimes we can rely on them and forget to trust in God alone to make worship happen.

We will return at the end of this chapter to see what happens after the disciples return. For now, let's just remember that Jesus was in the business of training and releasing his followers to do what he had been doing, and that we need to follow his example with our teams.

When team building goes sour

The final aspect of Jesus' team building that we want to highlight is found as part of his conversation during the last supper: 'Simon, Simon, Satan has asked to sift you as wheat. But I have prayed for you, Simon, that your faith may not fail. And when you have turned back, strengthen your brothers' (Luke 22:31–32).

We should notice here how Jesus has been praying for his core team as individuals: the Greek word used for 'you' is singular, implying specific prayer for Simon Peter.[6] We must make it a habit to pray specifically and regularly for our team members and those we mentor, asking God to speak to us about them, especially about any areas where they may be struggling.

In his times of prayer for Peter, Jesus has heard from the Father that the devil is out to entrap Peter. Peter hotly refutes the idea—and then goes on to deny Jesus three times (22:54–62). It is heartening to know that Jesus still loved Peter even though he knew he was going to let him down, and he still had a central role for Peter to play in his kingdom movement (John 21:15–19). This should encourage us when we fail, and it points to what our reaction should be when other people hurt or let us down. In all team and mentoring relationships, there will inevitably be times when we feel rejected or disappointed by the people in whom we invest.

At one time, Sam mentored a worship leader who was hard work: he would regularly miss rehearsal or training opportunities, and he led worship in ways that undermined our church ethos and made people feel uncomfortable. Sam stood by him, arguing that he should remain part of the team and investing time and effort trying to develop his gifts and confidence. There were times when Sam had to say 'no' to some ways he wanted to lead, or explain that his conduct was out of line. One day he snapped and sent a long letter of resignation, listing all the wrongs Sam had done him and the reasons why he was in no position to criticize him.

If you have been in a similar situation, you will know how devastating it can feel. Think how Jesus would have felt, standing across the courtyard and hearing Peter repeat three times, 'I do not know him' (22:56–62). Like Jesus, we must be prepared for rejection and disappointment from those we lead. More than that, we need to ask God for the strength to forgive people their mistakes, even if they do not apologize, and to reinstate those who genuinely ask for forgiveness and a second chance.

OUR AUTHORITY

Let's return to consider what happened after the disciples came back from their first mission trip. Although Luke 9 does not record how the disciples got on, we learn from Mark's version of events that they preached the gospel, cast out demons and healed sick people (Mark 6:12–13). Jesus has empowered and released them for ministry, and it is a success. On their return, he decides that they need a retreat together, but it is cut short by the crowds following them (Luke 9:10–11). The disciples are feeling fired up, full of enthusiasm, yet what follows is another classic example from them of messing up, in a way to which we can all relate.

It is hard to blame the disciples. Imagine for a moment that you are a steward at a big Christian event (fluorescent tabard, walkie talkie, the works) in one of those huge circus tents full of 5000 men, plus their wives and children. The speaker has been talking for ages, but at last he comes off stage and the worship band begins to play. Next moment, you realize that the speaker is heading towards you, and he has an expectant look in his eye.

'Steward, these people are hungry. You feed them.'

What would you do? Laugh? You would perhaps say, 'Well, the burger and doughnut vans have just closed for the day. I could go and try to find a supermarket, but it would have to be on expenses because feeding this lot will cost me six months' wages.'

He gives you a rather disappointed look, so you say, 'I'll see if there's anything left over from the stewards' tea.' You come back with three sandwiches, an apple and half a packet of smoky bacon crisps. 'This is all I could find…'

What were the disciples thinking when they showed Jesus five loaves and two fish? Were they having a laugh? 'Seriously, Jesus? How on earth are we going to do this?' Although they had only recently experienced success in their ministries, the disciples had forgotten three very important things.

First, they forgot what Jesus had promised them: 'Don't take food or money with you, God will provide' (see Luke 9:3); 'Blessed are you who hunger now, for you will be satisfied' (6:21); 'All things are possible with God' (Mark 10:27).

Second, they forgot not just his promises but his deeds. They had seen him heal people (Luke 5:12–13); Peter, James and John had seen him provide the miraculous catch of fish (5:1–11); they had seen him calm the storm (8:22–25). After all this, they still doubted his power over the simple matter of preparing some food. Are we any different? We, too, forget the answers to prayer we have received; we forget the miracles God does in our lives and the lives of others.

Third, they didn't just forget his promises and his deeds, but they forgot that he had given them authority in the spiritual realm. He was not asking them to work a miracle in their own strength—asking the impossible, which only he was capable of doing. No, the impossible things that he himself had done were the very things he had authorized his disciples to do. They had used this power in proclamation and healing, and now he was giving them the opportunity to use it in providing for the crowds. And they reverted to sarcasm, cynicism and unbelief: 'It's not possible, Jesus. We don't have the money, the resources... the... What? Look at all this bread and fish!'

In our ministry as leaders of worship, we will have times when Jesus asks us to do something that seems impossible: 'Lead these people in worship... Develop this team... reach this group of unbelievers'. Our natural instinct may be to give up hope, to become cynical and flippant. At these times, we must lift our eyes from the seemingly impossible task and remember Jesus' promises. We need to remember his deeds, in his life and in our own circumstances. And we need to remember that he has given us authority for all that he has called us to do. When we look at our task from that perspective, is our mission really so impossible?

⁜

Chapter 4

CREATIVE COMMUNICATOR

The small Baptist church where Sam spent his teenage years went through a phase of having a weekly five-minute 'kids' talk' in church each Sunday, just before the children went out to Sunday school. The memory of these little talks sticks in his head many years later, more than any of the hundreds of sermons or Bible studies he heard there. Why?

The reason is that they were creative. Lay people, who would not normally preach or lead, would think up illustrations with props, visual aids and audience participation to engage young and old with a focused, heartfelt thought. Although the talk was aimed at the children, often some of the adults would comment that it was their favourite part of the service. A simple point, creatively put, could speak directly into people's hearts.

Later, when we went to theological college, we were both involved with a 30-minute service started by our good friend Steve, at 10pm on a Tuesday night, called Lunar Eclipse.[1] This 'alternative' service explored reflective, multisensory approaches to engagement with God. We were also encouraged to facilitate creative worship in the college chapel services, and were inspired to share these experiences with others.

When we arrived at our previous church, Ascension, Sam's job was primarily about growing musical worship. Only a few weeks into his appointment, however, a visiting ministry team prophesied an 'explosion of creativity' in the church, and this resonated with what was going on in our hearts. When our senior leadership came back from a Willow Creek conference where they had seen creativity in action and excitedly asked if we could start a creative team, we jumped at the chance. This began a journey of growing volunteers, trying ideas, making mistakes, and taking steps of faith, which saw us engage with God in fresh and often surprising ways.

JESUS THE CREATIVE COMMUNICATOR

Sometimes, if we are overfamiliar with Jesus' teaching, we can focus on what he means and miss out on how he expresses it. As we work through Luke's Gospel, we should take a fresh look at the teaching style of Jesus, to see how he engages creatively with the people around him. Read Luke 13:18 and imagine him gazing into the middle distance as he dreams up fresh new ways of expressing the truth:

- 'What is the kingdom of God like? What shall I compare it to?' (NIV)
- 'How can I picture God's kingdom for you? What kind of story can I use?' (*THE MESSAGE*)
- 'What is the Kingdom of God like? How can I illustrate it?' (NLT)

He is grasping for a simple, contemporary metaphor, something the peasant people around him will be able to relate to, and yet at the same time something profound. Then it hits him: 'It is like a mustard seed, which a man took and planted in his garden. It grew and became a tree, and the birds of the air perched in its branches' (v. 19).

Jesus uses a mustard seed, an everyday object, familiar to all his hearers—although, in his telling, he adds a few twists to the scenario which may not be immediately apparent to us but would have struck his original listeners.

First, in those days, you planted mustard seeds in fields, not gardens.[2] Is Jesus suggesting that his kingdom will be 'planted' in unfamiliar places? Even more potent is his reference to 'the birds of the air', a common Old Testament image for all the peoples of the earth (see Daniel 4:12, 21; Ezekiel 17:23; 31:6).[3] This kingdom, although planted as a small, insignificant thing in unlikely places, will grow huge and draw in everybody, everywhere. So Jesus uses a simple, familiar image with powerful and resonant significance.

Jesus was a storyteller, a speaker of parables and proverbs, and a very creative one at that. His parables varied depending on his audience: to rich people he spoke of business and finance (Luke 12:13–21); to those who thought themselves righteous he told tales of judgment (18:9–14); to large crowds he used familiar farming metaphors (8:4–8). He could use current events, the news of the day, to teach about the ways of God (13:1–5). He could develop an idea using a trilogy of images, building his point as in the stories of the lost sheep, the lost coin and, most dramatically, the lost son (see Luke 15).

Although storytelling seems to have been Jesus' main gift, he could also employ visual aids. When asked, 'Who is the greatest?' he drew a young child into the circle—a striking, tangible image of humility (9:46–48). When people tried to trap him with questions about taxes, he asked them to hold up a Roman coin, and the picture of Caesar helped him sidestep the snare (20:20–26). Most importantly, he used the everyday physical symbols of bread and wine to initiate the most significant act of Christian worship in history, Holy Communion (22:17–20). We will look at this particular act in more depth at the end of the chapter.

We have already discussed the notion that worship is far more than just music, and that in recent times we have perhaps forgotten this truth, so that 'a time of worship' implies a time of singing and not much else. Of course, you may be thinking, 'But music is creative', and you're right. There is so much musical creativity that remains untapped in our churches if we stick to a narrow selection of music. When was the last time you used a song outside your tradition, which challenged your normal playing style? Personally we have found it invigorating for our bands and congregations when we try new musical forms—for example, adding jazz chord substitutions and swung rhythms to a well-known chorus, or using a electronic drum loop to add a 'dance' music feel to a familiar song. We have, on occasion, played something in the style of a well-known pop or rock song (including 'I will worship' to the riff from 'Love machine' by Girls Aloud), bringing new life to it. We have also explored songs from Africa and Latin America, as they encourage us to play outside our usual rhythms and chords, and we've used orchestral instruments to attempt a more classical feel. Perhaps after reading this chapter, you may be inspired to work to develop your musical vocabulary by learning some new chords or grooves, listening to other styles of music and incorporating more variety into your church's musical diet.

Yet music is only a part of the potential creativity that could be used in your services. Stop and think about your own church, and your own experience of worship. Have you worshipped in other ways than simply singing or praying? Do non-musicians have any input into the worship life of the church? What other art forms are used in your fellowship to help people engage with God—flower arranging, video editing, dance, rap, drama, visual art?[4]

WHY DEVELOP CREATIVE WORSHIP?

Why does creativity matter? Why should we encourage other forms of expression and communication in our corporate worship? Let's leave Luke for a moment and reflect on the reasons why creativity is, in fact, vitally important for the development of Western 21st-century Christian worship:

The days we live in

We live in a time of unprecedented growth in creative communication. As the printing press facilitated the intellectual and religious cultural shift of the Renaissance and the Reformation, so television and, more recently, computers and the Internet have enabled a communication revolution in our society. How much are we prepared to engage with this revolution as far as our church life is concerned?

Television engages us through colour, movement, symbols and sound—complex patterns of signs which we process and understand rapidly and instinctively. For example, watch the TV news. After a quick introduction, they will cut to an interview or an eyewitness video or a moving graphic. Other genres of TV and film also make hugely creative use of music and sound, lighting and editing to create effects and build a mood.

The Internet has taken this kind of communication to a new level, giving everyone the chance to share their creativity. People can make videos, record songs or write blogs and instantly share them with the world. There are probably people in your church who are familiar with video editing software, who take beautiful digital photographs or can do creative things with PowerPoint. In fact, children and teenagers can be more skilled in these areas than adults.

Will a 30-minute spoken sermon keep people's attention compared to a news broadcast? Will singing a song be able to paint a more powerful picture of God than images we might see in a film?

Some people may object that if we use such media and art forms, we cannot avoid importing 'worldly' or unbiblical values along with them. Does a service complete with video clips, a live rock band, PowerPoint presentations and other contemporary art forms become simply dumbed-down, self-help entertainment?

The truth is that often our starting point is wrong. We begin by attempting to compete with or copy the world. We rush in to use contemporary technology and art forms uncritically, without thinking through the biblical view of creativity, and we end up frustrated and compromised. Ultimately we are in danger of a form of idolatry, where the art form takes centre stage rather than Jesus. Instead, we need to face the challenges of contemporary communication from a biblical standpoint, asking what God's word and, ultimately, the life and teaching of Jesus show us about these issues. Then we can engage with them in a way that honours him.

Biblical mandate for creativity

The Bible is full of creative engagement with God. There isn't the space here to go into detail about God's beautiful, symbolic design for the tabernacle and its furnishings (Exodus 25—28), the singing and dancing of the Israelites (Exodus 15:20; 1 Chronicles 25; 2 Samuel 6:13–15) or the dramatized actions of the prophets (Ezekiel 4; Jeremiah 19:1–13), but reading just a few of these passages should make it clear to us that God expects us to approach him through the full range of creativity that he has given to us as a gift.[5] Often, people have misinterpreted the second commandment (Exodus 20:4) as meaning that the Israelites were to make no images at all, when in fact the restriction is against making an idol, an object of worship.[6] Visual or creative aids to worship must only point us towards worshipping the ultimate Creator; they are never to be worshipped or exalted themselves.

Most importantly, it is in Jesus that we find our ultimate example of sanctified creativity. He is the one in whom we find out what it means for humankind to be made in the image of God (Genesis 1:26; Colossians 1:15). In Jesus, we see humankind as it is supposed to be. At the same time, we see God through tangible, graspable human experience. By redeeming and sanctifying our humanity, Jesus also makes the way for our redeemed creativity, showing us how we might 'image God' in our lives, attitudes and expressions of worship. As John says, 'That which was from the beginning, which we have *heard*, which we have *seen with our eyes*, which we have *looked at* and our hands have *touched*—this we proclaim concerning the Word of life' (1 John 1:1, our emphasis).

What a mandate for us—to follow in the footsteps of those who first encountered Jesus, in making the eternal Word of God known to people in ways they can hear, see with their eyes, look at and touch. We should be inspired by our encounters with Jesus to make art that brings heaven to earth. As William Dryness, professor of theology and culture at Fuller Theological Seminary, puts it, 'This experience for the Christian is grounded in the fact that God himself became part of the creation in Jesus Christ, and as we are rooted and grounded in Christ, the power of the Holy Spirit enables us to shape lives (and materials) in ways that bring glory to God.'[7]

The limitations of music

The third reason why creativity is so important for our worship is that there are limits to what corporate singing can achieve. Speaking personally, we are musical worship leaders first and foremost; we love church singing and believe that it is probably the primary medium for helping a group of people to join together to engage with God. Yet it is far from being the only way.

Some people simply cannot sing; we have had people in our church who were profoundly tone deaf, and one who had tinnitus, which made all music sound like ringing alarm bells. Others simply do not enjoy singing, or find it a strange and alien experience, given their background. While we want to help such people develop an appreciation for song,[8] as servants of the whole church we should be considering other ways in which people can worship.

Joining together to sing is an excellent way of expressing certain parts of worship—praise and adoration, proclaiming who God is and the greatness of his majesty—but some aims are perhaps better served by other media. For example, lament is hard to get right in a time of corporate song. Instead, why not encourage people to write a lament prayer on a piece of paper and stick it to a cross, while a solo instrument, such as a cello, plays a mournful tune? Perhaps images of the situation you are lamenting can be projected on to a screen. Using a combination of image, music and action can be a far more appropriate and powerful way of expressing lament for a church community.

While corporate song is an excellent way of making a community response, what about the times when you want people to have an individual, personal reaction to a talk or time of sung worship? Art corners, with simple materials, some suggestions printed on the walls and quiet space for reflection, can provide a helpful way for people to express themselves before God. A number of times, we have encouraged whole congregations to take 20 minutes at the end of a talk to respond using art materials. Before they started, we explained that God loves their creative expressions even if they don't consider them to be very 'good', just as every parent loves the messy paintings their child offers. It has been thrilling to see the very young, the very old and all ages in between take up the challenge, the paintbrush and pencil, and have a go.

This is not to say that creative worship cannot be corporate. On one occasion, when our theme was the body of Christ, we outlined a huge human body on the floor of the church with masking tape (a striking and intriguing image for people to see as they walked in) and invited everyone to take their place, standing within the 'body', as we sang together. Sometimes creative worship could involve an element of performance—a drama team, a choreographed dance or the performance of a piece of music. It is always important to follow this with an opportunity for the congregation to respond together, so that the service is participatory and not simply a 'show'.

Another limitation of music-based worship is that it generally uses only one of our senses—that of hearing. God gave us five senses and it is probably right to assume that he wants us to use all of them in worship. Our next passage from Luke's Gospel offers an example of someone worshipping Jesus in a multisensory way.

A creative, extravagant offering

Luke 7:36–50 records the actions of a 'sinful' woman (she was most probably a prostitute[9]), who comes in repentance to Jesus for the life she has been living. The fact that she was a woman was reason enough, in that culture, for Jesus to ignore her presence at the table; her 'reputation' would have made his acknowledgment of her even more shocking to the guests. It seems that her tearful repentance turns into an act of worship and adoration as she discovers Jesus' loving acceptance. Simon the Pharisee is too busy judging her, and Jesus as well, to see that it is he who is sinning—neglecting to provide Jesus with foot-washing and ignoring his own need for forgiveness.

Then [Jesus] turned toward the woman and said to Simon, 'Do you see this woman? I came into your house. You did not give me any water for my feet, but she wet my feet with her tears and wiped them with her hair. You did not give me a kiss, but this woman, from the time I entered, has not stopped kissing my feet. You did not put oil on my head, but she has poured perfume on my feet. Therefore, I tell you, her many sins have been forgiven—for she loved much. But the one who has been forgiven little loves little' (vv. 44–47).

This story should raise questions about our own attitude towards worshipping Jesus. If we are aware of the extent to which we have been forgiven, and that we are 'loved much' by Jesus, do we respond by 'loving much' with extravagant offerings of worship? Do we do the minimum possible in the preparation and execution of services, or are we prepared to pour out the best of our effort for Jesus?

In John's account of a similar story (John 12:1–8), Judas complains that the money the woman spent on the perfume could have been given to the poor, but John adds that he said this only because he was greedy (v. 6). Have we ever been guilty of scrimping financially or in the use of our gifts in our worship of Jesus? This is not to say that all worship should be a lavish, glitzy show, but it should be costly. Jesus paid the ultimate price for us; are we prepared to show him a similar kind of devotion?

The woman in the story worshipped Jesus not by singing to him but by offering him the best, most precious thing she had—expensive perfume, worth far more than the oil that Simon couldn't be bothered to give Jesus. Imagine how intoxicating the smell of the perfume must have been as it filled the room. In addition, she offered her tears, her hair, her hands, her lips—a tactile and intimate expression of adoration.

 WORSHIP IDEAS

If sung worship is limited because it uses only one of our senses, how can we make our worship multisensory? Here are a few ideas that we have tried.[10]

- **Taste:** Give out spoons of honey and glasses of cold water. Encourage people to reflect on the song lyric 'Your name is like honey on my lips, your Spirit like water to my soul' from 'Jesus, Jesus, holy and anointed one',[11] while actually experiencing those tastes. Use food from around the world in worship to remind people that we are part of a global church.
- **Touch:** Provide large, rough nails for people to hold as they consider Jesus on the cross. Hand out modelling clay and ask people to work it into a pot while considering the image of God as a potter, shaping our lives (Isaiah 64:8). Give out bricks while talking about Nehemiah rebuilding the walls of Jerusalem, invite people to write their names on them with marker pens and build a wall representing your whole church.

- **Smell**: Use Revelation 8:3–4 to talk about our prayers rising as incense to God, while burning some incense sticks or lighting a censer. Provide perfume to help people consider the woman's extravagant offering of praise in Luke 7:36–50. Use a bad smell and a beautiful scent to contrast the 'fragrance of life' with the 'fragrance of death' that 2 Corinthians 2:15–16 talks about.
- **Sight**: Use slides of appropriate visual art for people to meditate on, or ask someone to make an original piece for you.[12] It could be figurative art or something more abstract. Print out images of Christ from many different cultures and eras, and collage them on a large cardboard outline of the world or the risen Christ.
- **Hearing**: Use sound effects to enhance a Bible reading, such as thunder and lightning followed by gentle waves for the calming of the storm (Luke 8:22–25), or, if you have skilled musicians, ask them to interpret the reading instrumentally as it is spoken. Play live or CD instrumental music to help people meditate on a text or thought.[13] Use poetry, rap or other spoken-word performance.[14]

Multisensory worship helps to engage the whole person and express more of who God is. It affirms our humanity and can release worship in ways that singing alone cannot do. You may be thinking that this all sounds time-consuming, difficult to introduce, or too far outside your own experience and expertise. Remember the effort of the 'sinful' (or, as we should probably say, the 'forgiven') woman as she worshipped Jesus in a fitting response to all he had done for her. Surely we should be prepared to make a similar kind of costly, creative, extravagant offering.

Don't forget, though, that a lot of creative worship can be very simple. We consider some of the practical questions about developing creative kinds of worship at the end of this chapter.

Meanwhile, here is a worship experience that offers an example of how simple and yet profound such worship can be.

WORSHIP EXPERIENCE

Find a pile of old magazines or newspapers, a sheet of plain paper and some glue. Go through the magazines, ripping out pictures or headlines that help express a part of your relationship with God. Include both the positive and negative, and be as honest as you like. Arrange the torn-out items on the sheet of paper as a prayerful, worshipful collage for God.

A friend of ours led this activity in our home group with a varied group of people. We wondered if some members would enjoy the process and were pleasantly surprised to see everyone, including those who were not normally 'creative', really get into it.

PERPLEXING PARABLES

Before we continue unpacking the theme of Jesus' creativity, we need to take a look at one of Jesus' more confusing comments about his use of parables. He has just told the parable of the sower (Luke 8:4–8), and his disciples ask him about its meaning. He replies, 'The knowledge of the secrets of the kingdom of God has been given to you, but to others I speak in parables, so that, "though seeing, they may not see; though hearing, they may not understand"' (v. 10).

What does Jesus mean here? We have talked about the parables as everyday metaphors, which ordinary people can understand. Is he implying the opposite here—that he chooses to obscure his message from those whom he does not want to believe it? Are parables, and other creative forms of communication, actually more of a barrier to faith than a bridge? Should we restrict ourselves to 'plain speaking'?

We need to see this verse in the context in which Luke places it. The parable of the sower, which precedes this statement, demonstrates that the farmer wants his entire crop to grow[15] (which farmer wouldn't?) but there is a certain inevitability that some seed will not fall in good soil. Unusually, Jesus explains his parable. The seed is the word of God. God desires for all to grow and bear fruit, but knows that the devil and the cares of the world will get in the way of many growing into fullness of life in him (vv. 11–14).

Jesus stresses a number of times in this passage that the quality of the person's hearing is the deciding factor, not the quality of the seed or its method of distribution: 'Those who have ears to hear, let them hear... Therefore consider carefully how you listen' (vv. 8, 18).

If we choose to listen to God's word, however it is proclaimed, with the intention of knowing him better, God will reveal more to us by the Holy Spirit: 'whoever has [this attitude] will be given more' (v. 18), and 'the secrets of the kingdom of God' will be revealed to us (v. 10). Jesus never intends for the light he shines to be hidden under a bowl or a bed (vv. 16–17).[16] But if our soil, our heart, is not open to go deeper with him—if we don't listen with the intention of hearing his deeper message—we will hear no more than words or stories.[17]

The parables, rather than being a blockage to understanding, function to draw out the contrast between different types of listening. Like all good art, poetry or music, the parables offer not merely an explanation but an experience of something higher, deeper, more transcendent, if only we are prepared to engage with them. But, as we have seen, they also allow people to ignore the hidden meaning. As Marshall says:

By this method of teaching in parables Jesus not only invited his audiences to penetrate below the surface and find the real meaning; at the same time he allowed them opportunity—which many of them took—of turning a blind eye and a deaf ear to the real point of the issue.[18]

As we consider using stories, visuals or other art forms in our worship and services, in a sense we offer a similar opportunity for our congregations. These expressions should never replace the word of God spoken and preached with clarity. At the same time, they offer a complementary opportunity for people to engage and respond to God's word in a more interactive format, with media 'whose meaning does not lie on the surface, but demands enquiry and insight'.[19] As R.T. France goes on to say, 'To understand a parable is usually to be changed.' Some people will be hostile to new forms of worship (but then some people always are...) or will perhaps be unable to engage as well as others can with worship that requires creative thinking and a different level of response. For many others, however, if we take them by the hand and lead them on a journey with the Holy Spirit as their guide, new expressions of worship will expand their horizons and draw them into a deeper experience of and response to God.

A final application from the parable of the sower comes from Tom Wright: 'What can we do to plough up the rough ground, to remove the stones, to weed out the thorns? What can we do to sow the word more successfully?'[20]

There may be a challenge here for our use of creativity in evangelism as well as worship. Do we sometimes preach the gospel to people whose hearts and lives are not ready to receive it? Of course, there are other ways to 'prepare the ground': if people see Christians serving the poor and disadvantaged, living lives of loving fellowship, being friendly and approachable rather than 'holier than thou', these attitudes should all help to bring down barriers of prejudice and improve receptivity to the gospel. But the arts may also have a role to play.

In our previous church, we ran termly 'café style' evenings, where people could bring their non-Christian friends. Each night featured some live music, a talk on a contemporary theme and other creative media to engage the audience in thinking though the topic from a Christian perspective. So we had Radiohead and U2 nights, with covers bands, video projection, art installations and talks about how these artists' views agreed or contrasted with the biblical worldview. We had a 'Divine comedy' night, with a professional Christian stand-up comedian, comedy sketches and a talk about God's attitude towards humour. There was a 'Life is jazz' evening, with a jazz pianist taking us through the history of the genre, a video and a talk about how our lives should be an 'improvisation' on the 'theme' God gives us.

These evenings always ended with some sort of opportunity for reflection and meditation, perhaps using PowerPoint, instrumental music or the chance for people to discuss their reactions at their tables. No direct gospel invitation was given but the nights helped non-Christian guests to think about God in new ways, relevant to their lives. Creative use of a range of art forms perhaps 'cleared some ground' of negative assumptions about who God is and what is important to Christians. We are not suggesting that you copy the format of these evenings, but you could think about what might be relevant in your situation, what gifts in your church could be used in a similar event, and what local people might consider to be a worthwhile night out.

BACK TO THE TABLE

Once, Sam was preparing a time of Sunday worship. He had spent quite a bit of time thinking through the theme, considering the congregation, praying and listening to God, and had put together a set of songs that he felt fitted well together. Just as he was about to go on to another task, he looked at the monthly rota and noticed something about the coming service that would upset all his plans. 'Flipping Communion,' he muttered under his breath.

Almost as soon as the words were out of his mouth, he was horrified at what he had just said. He literally got down on his knees in his office in repentance for what he had said, but, more importantly, for the idea that his planned song set was more important than the one act of worship commanded of us by Jesus—the act where we celebrate his precious blood spilt and body broken for our sinfulness. Sam repented for his selfish, arrogant ways.

It may sound shocking to some, but it may well be the case that many worship leaders have been guilty of a similar attitude towards the Lord's supper. It gets in the way of the nice long worship time. It demands that we pick from a certain group of songs. Perhaps the use of the Communion table involves moving the musical gear and fitting into a smaller space—how inconvenient!

Perhaps we need to look again at Communion, to remember what it is really about and to draw it back into the centre of our worship, rather than allowing it to be something that is merely tacked on to the end of a service.[21] We should remember that Jesus shared his last supper on Passover night (Luke 22:14–20), one of the most important festivals in the Jewish calendar. It was the time when people remembered the blood of the sacrificial lamb placed on the doors of their houses so that the angel of death would 'pass over' them, and their subsequent escape from slavery in Egypt. Jesus himself does not draw this parallel but it must have been in the minds of those reflecting on events at the time.[22] Even before Jesus' death, the meal was potent with symbolism.

Jesus takes the symbolism further, however. It was traditional for the youngest son (note God's concern for people of all ages to understand) to ask the father of the household questions about the significance of the night and the food they were eating.[23] Jesus uses these 'teaching moments' to load the symbolic elements of bread and wine with even more meaning: '"This is my body given for you; do this in remembrance of me." In the same way, after the supper he took the cup, saying, "This cup is the new covenant in my blood, which is poured out for you"' (vv. 19–20). Jesus takes the familiar elements and applies them to himself; affirming their existing significance but also taking it further and centring them on his imminent death.

The use of the phrase 'new covenant' holds far more weight than we usually appreciate. The 'old covenant' between God and Abraham (Genesis 15), sealed in blood by Moses (Exodus 24:8), was central to the Jewish faith. It was staggering for Jesus to proclaim himself the bearer of the new covenant—promised by the prophet Jeremiah (31:31–34), when the Law would be written on people's hearts and young and old would know the Lord personally. The significance of Jesus' powerful use of the bread and wine was made plain to those with 'ears to hear', to the extent that the disciples continued this meal as the central act of early church worship (1 Corinthians 11:23–26; Acts 2:42).

We must somehow break through our overfamiliarity with the Lord's supper, to come at it afresh. Perhaps the traditions we have built around it, although not bad in themselves, have made it stale. The repetition of the same liturgical words may have dulled our minds to the fantastic truths they proclaim, or the notion of it being a meal of 'remembrance' might have distracted us from Communion as a place where we can experience God himself. As James Torrance writes:

The trinitarian view sees the Lord's supper as the supreme expression of all worship. It is the act in which the risen and ascended Lord meets us at his table, in the power of the Spirit, to bring his passion to our remembrance, and to draw us to himself that we may share his communion with the Father and his intercessions for the world.[24]

This is an incredibly exciting meal! We are supposed to celebrate Communion—to encounter Jesus as he offers himself and us to the Father, by the Spirit; to join around the table as brothers and sisters, as equals, to proclaim his gracious death for us until he comes again. So how can we use our creativity to enhance our celebration of Communion?

WORSHIP IDEAS

Here are some different ideas that may be helpful in re-envisioning the Communion service. You may need to talk things through with your church leader, but most should be open to new ideas, even if you have to include them alongside your existing traditions.

- We have used a variety of international breads—naans, focaccia, pitta, rye, baguettes and whatever else you can find—to remember that we represent a worldwide Church.
- We have placed the table in the middle of the church and encouraged people to serve each other, as a sign that we are family.
- We have been involved in an 'Emmaus Communion' (inspired by the story in Luke 24:13–33), where people walk up to the table in pairs, discussing what God has done in their lives recently. They then walk away together, talking about what they feel God is calling them to do in the future.
- You could celebrate a 'covenant feast' using the liturgy in Appendix 2, written by Ruth Neve. This should be a lively service with joyful songs, in contrast to the usual sombre mood of a Communion time.
- We heard of one church where they placed bread makers around the room on timers, so that the bread baked as the service went on, and at the end everyone shared in fresh loaves. (Imagine the smell!)
- We have also used film clips to introduce the meal, such as the scene from *The Mission*[25] where Robert de Niro struggles up the mountain with a huge pack on his back, trying to pay penance for the sin of killing his brother. As he reaches

the top, it is not the act of penance that saves him but the grace shown to him by those he has been mistreating—the native people of the island—who cut him both literally and symbolically free from his burdens and accept him into their community. We ask people to consider their burdens. What are they trying to carry to earn God's forgiveness? Then we pray that they may allow Jesus to take that burden, because he is the one we have wronged, and he takes our sins and sets us free.

Everyday objects

As well as occupying a central place in worship, the Lord's Supper also challenges us to think through our use of creativity and symbolism in worship. Jesus took ordinary, everyday elements, bread and wine, and used them to express the truths of his kingdom. How can we use what people interact with each day—mobile phones, chocolate and coffee, plant pots—and turn them into parables, signs or illustrations of the kingdom and signposts to worship?

- Turn off all the lights to make the church as dark as you can. Then ask people to switch on their mobile phones, using just this faint light to reflect on John 1:5: 'The light shines in the darkness, but the darkness has not overcome it.'
- Hand out Fairtrade coffee beans and chocolate and ask people to eat them while reflecting on the bitterness of unfair trade. Then think about the sweetness of justice and pray for God to be at work in these issues.
- Provide plant pots, soil, seed and water. Encourage people to meditate on John 12:24, plant the seed and then consider that in their own lives they need the water of the Spirit, the light of God, and the feeding of his word to enable them

to grow. They can take the pots home as a reminder of the service.

The ideas above can work well as prayer stations around the church. This involves setting up a space (or a number of different spaces) in the church with instructions and props, and inviting people to use them in a worship time or as a response. The stations can be themed to your service, or more general. Each station should:

- engage at least one of the senses.
- offer some simple, clear instructions.
- include a scripture passage or two for people to reflect on.
- lead people through a simple meditation or prayer.

Stations are good because people can move around and engage as much or as little as they like with each one. We usually play quiet music to create a reflective atmosphere and invite people to interact with the stations or just sit in God's presence or read their Bibles. This means that nobody feels left out if they do not want to take part.

DRAWING ON TRADITION

We have seen that Jesus used everyday objects in worship, but also that he respected and drew from the Jewish spiritual tradition in which he had been raised. Are we in danger of ignoring 2000 years of Christian tradition in favour of always looking for the 'latest sensation'? Have you ever used Celtic liturgy[26] or a prayer from the early Church, or a quote from Luther or Calvin, to focus people on God in a fresh way? Are we aware of songs from around the world,[27] which might express worship differently? How often do we draw on the historic creeds to express what we believe?

All these ideas are tried and tested, and we have found that they help people draw closer to God. You can think up more for your own situation. It is not so hard to get started; this final section will give you some tips on applying these thoughts in your context.

MAKING A START

Introducing creative worship in your church should be more about evolution than revolution. We personally don't call it 'alternative worship'[28] because we don't believe that it is just for a small niche of people: everyone has been made by God to respond creatively, through more than just music. Often, however, you will need to 'drip feed' something new into the service to get people used to it gradually. This is where we have found the 'movements of worship' planning style outlined in Appendix 1 useful. You can have a normal service, with a recognizable format, but introduce something creative in, say, the intercessions or the call to worship or the Bible reading. Then people will understand it in context and it will be surrounded by other more familiar movements of worship. As we gradually introduced more creative elements into our services, people became more and more comfortable with the idea of worshipping in multisensory ways.

Build a team

We talked about Jesus' team building in the previous chapter. You may feel completely inexperienced or unqualified to lead this kind of worship, but consider the people you have in your church. Are there artists, poets, dancers or teachers who might be itching to get involved? Spread the word that you are looking for people, and you might be surprised what kind of gifts are hiding in your church. Look for people with some experience, especially if you are just starting out, but also for amateurs who are willing to learn.

Invest

Despite what some may assume, creative worship doesn't have to cost very much: household objects such as stones, pencils, candles and food can all help us worship God with very little expenditure. If you want to take it seriously, however, it is worth asking your church for a budget for props and materials. If a group of people wants to develop an area like video, visual art or dance, they may need to invest in equipment or training opportunities. Most of all, invest as much time as you can in discussion, rehearsal and preparation. Try to 'dress rehearse' any performed pieces or items that use complex technology, as it can be very distracting (not to say frustrating) when foreseeable problems crop up.

Pray

Creative worship is just as 'spiritual' as any other activity, but sometimes it is easy to forget to include God when we are busy preparing or rehearsing. The next chapter explores how we can learn to rely more upon God's presence and power in worship, seeking to be more fully reliant on the Holy Spirit. Pray with your team before and/or after a rehearsal or preparation time, making use of their creative gifts in your prayers. Listen to God for direction and creative ideas, and support one another in prayer between meetings by keeping in contact through email or text message. Hold the tension between preparation and growing in your natural gifts on the one hand and, on the other hand, depending on God to breathe life into your art so that it can have eternal significance.

✜

Chapter 5

RELIANT ON THE SPIRIT

If you are not a raving, hands-down-for-coffee charismatic, you might be tempted to skip this chapter. But the Holy Spirit is not just some kind of accessory for a certain type of Christian, like a rainbow guitar strap, a fish car sticker, or a 'What Would Jesus Do?' bracelet. He is at the core of our faith and at the heart of all Christian worship. This chapter explores how Jesus' life in Luke can inspire us to truly Spirit-filled worship.

In Chapter 1 we discussed the fact that although Jesus was fully God, he was also fully human and thus had to be fully reliant on the Holy Spirit to live a life of perfect worship. This means that every act he did was a trinitarian act—Jesus the Son, doing the will of the Father, by the Holy Spirit. As Peter explains in the book of Acts, 'God anointed Jesus of Nazareth with the Holy Spirit and power, and... he went around doing good and healing all who were under the power of the devil, because God was with him' (10:38).

Luke mentions the Holy Spirit more than any other Gospel writer, demonstrating how Jesus was fully reliant on the Holy Spirit. He did not bring himself to the earth but was conceived by the Spirit (1:35), the Spirit anointed him at his baptism (3:22), he was led and empowered by the Holy Spirit during his temptation in the desert (4:1, 14), and he proclaimed that the Spirit was at the very core of his identity and mission, anointing him to preach and heal (vv. 18–19). The book of Hebrews shows us that on the cross he offered himself by the Spirit, presenting a perfect sacrifice, unlike the old system involving 'the blood of goats and calves' (9:12): 'How much more, then, will the blood of Christ, who *through the eternal Spirit* offered himself unblemished to God, cleanse our consciences from acts that lead to death, so that we may serve the living God!' (v. 14, emphasis added).

Even in his resurrection, the Bible says, Jesus was raised by the Father through the Spirit (Romans 1:4; 8:11). But the truly amazing thing about Romans 8:9–11 is that it proclaims that the Spirit of Christ—the same Spirit who empowered Jesus' perfect life of worship and raised Christ from the dead—is not limited to Jesus but can be found in us (see also Ephesians 1:18–20). We can be filled with that same presence of God to join in Jesus' worship of the Father. All Christians have the Spirit of Christ inside them, every act of Christian worship is 'in the Spirit', and the deeper we delve into this knowledge, the more we will be released to worship as Jesus leads us.

We need to bring the Holy Spirit in from the periphery of church worship, to stop seeing him as being concerned only with charismatic phenomena and manifestations. We need to remember always that just as he empowered Jesus for a life of perfect worship, so he wants to empower us too, to be like Jesus in our lives and acts of worship.

THE SPIRIT AS THE 'DYNAMIS' OF GOD

'One day Jesus was teaching, and Pharisees and teachers of the law were sitting there. They had come from every village of Galilee and from Judea and Jerusalem. And *the power of the Lord was with Jesus* to heal those who were ill' (Luke 5:17, TNIV, emphasis added).

This is an introductory verse to the great story about Jesus healing the paralysed man who was lowered through the roof. It explains that the power of God was present in Jesus to do acts of healing. The word for 'power' here is the Greek word *dynamis*, from which we get words like 'dynamic' and 'dynamite'. It's the same word used in Luke 24:19, when the disciples on the road to Emmaus describes Jesus as 'a prophet, powerful in word and deed', and then in verse 49, where the disciples are commanded by Jesus, 'Stay in the city until you have been clothed with power from on high.' With Acts 2 at the back of our minds, we know that this 'power from on high' was to be the Holy Spirit.

From Luke 5:17 it should be clear, then, that Jesus did not muster up in himself some power to heal. It is the Holy Spirit who makes possible the presence of God's power on earth. Theologian Luke Timothy Johnson translates the last sentence in this verse as 'The power of the Lord was enabling him to heal.'[1] Jesus was, as we have stressed before, fully God, but he limited himself to live as fully human, and for that reason he relied on the Holy Spirit to do his acts of kingdom power.

If that was true for Jesus, how much more should we rely fully on the Spirit, to live lives of worship and to lead others? And yet how often do we forget to take the time to welcome him into our hearts and our services?

In Acts, Luke gives us a fuller report of Jesus' final words to the disciples: 'Do not leave Jerusalem, but wait for the gift my Father promised, which you have heard me speak about. For John baptized with water, but in a few days you will be baptized with the Holy Spirit' (Acts 1:4–5). Probably the hardest word for us to hear in that passage is 'wait'. We are often so eager to rush into times of worship leading, relying on rehearsal, musical skill, the PA system and the words on the screen, but how often do we take time to wait upon God, to rely upon his Spirit?

A few years ago, we went away on a church weekend. It was a busy time, as we had to load tons of equipment into a van and spend hours rigging, sound checking and rehearsing around the packed schedule of meetings and meals. Everything looked and sounded great but, somewhere towards the end of the weekend, Sam began to feel uneasy. He realized he was choosing songs less for their relevance or because of God's leading, and more because he felt they would 'work'—inspiring hand-raising, loud singing or some other reaction from the congregation. He realized that not once over the whole weekend had we prayed together as a music group, and as a result he felt as if the worship had been empty and shallow.

These concerns about our church worship were confirmed when, a week later, two women grabbed Sara after she had just led the time of singing. 'Sara!' they gushed. 'Your singing was so wonderful today! We didn't feel like we needed to sing ourselves at all. We were just caught up in the sound of your voice!' The alarm bells rang louder in our heads. Were we relying on our technology and skills so much, and the Holy Spirit so little, that our worship had become a shallow performance?

We knew that drastic measures were called for, so, for the next few months (which coincidentally ran into Lent), we stripped down all our singing in services to simple songs accompanied by just a guitar or piano. Meanwhile, we turned our weekly band practice over to a 90-minute prayer time, to seek God, ask his forgiveness and pray for the worship life of the church. We invited the Holy Spirit to fill us once again, that we might be led by him to worship the Father through what Jesus has done. We intentionally put our reliance back on him to bring depth and life to our worship.

When we eventually reinstated our bands for Easter, the results of the prayer were clearly apparent, as was the effect on our congregations of getting used to worship without a band. Worship was more of a corporate act than an individual performance. We weren't trying to manipulate anyone or second-guess God's will, but let his Spirit take control. It is a lesson that we have to keep coming back to, to humble ourselves before God, telling him that we are totally reliant on his Holy Spirit to bring life and meaning to our worship.

 WORSHIP EXPERIENCE

Write down on a piece of paper all the things you think you may rely on in place of the Holy Spirit, both in your everyday life and in your worship leading. What earthly things do you find security in—money, technology, natural talents, your job title or position, people? Ask God for forgiveness where you have not trusted in him.

Then spend some time meditating on this edited version of the *Veni, Creator Spiritus,* an ancient prayer attributed to the monk and theologian Rabanus Maurus (776–856). Ask the Holy Spirit to fill you, forgive your sins and empower you to trust God.

> *Come, Holy Spirit, Creator blest,*
> *and in our souls take up Thy rest;*
> *come with Thy grace and heavenly aid*
> *to fill the hearts which Thou hast made.*
>
> *O comforter, to Thee we cry,*
> *O heavenly gift of God Most High,*
> *O fount of life and fire of love,*
> *and sweet anointing from above.*
>
> *Kindle our sense from above,*
> *and make our hearts o'erflow with love;*
> *with patience firm and virtue high*
> *the weakness of our flesh supply.*
>
> *Now to the Father and the Son,*
> *Who rose from death, be glory given,*
> *with Thou, O Holy Comforter,*
> *henceforth by all in earth and heaven. Amen*

WORSHIPPING BY THE SPIRIT

In Luke 10:17–24, we see an example of Jesus worshipping 'in the Spirit'. Sometimes, when people use the phrase 'Spirit-filled worship', what they seem to mean is either something totally unplanned (and possibly chaotic), or a time when a certain mood of peace and calm is achieved in the room. Although we are in no position to judge these people, we might venture to make a couple of comments about their assumptions.

First, as we have discovered, all Christian worship must be empowered by the Spirit (see Philippians 3:3), whether it's planned or spontaneous, and whether or not we get a warm glow from it. Sometimes, what is called a 'Spirit-filled' approach to worship can have a lot more to do with the musical preferences of the worshipper than the Holy Spirit.

With that in mind, however, it is still the case that at certain times during worship the Holy Spirit makes himself known in more obvious ways. Perhaps the best-known biblical example is in Acts 4:31, where the disciples are worshipping and the whole place is shaken by the Spirit. But of course we also see it in the life of Jesus: 'At that time Jesus, full of joy through the Holy Spirit, said, "I praise you, Father, Lord of heaven and earth"' (Luke 10:21). Tom Wright translates these words, 'There and then Jesus celebrated in the Holy Spirit',[2] while another commentator explains that '"in the Holy Spirit" here means "under the influence of" the Holy Spirit'.[3] There is no doubt that Jesus' worship, as described in this passage, was especially inspired by the Spirit as he was filled with joy to celebrate God's goodness.

It is encouraging to see that this Spirit-infilling for special times of worship is not limited to Jesus. Luke uses very similar words to speak of both Elizabeth and Mary, who are filled with joy by the Holy Spirit at the news of Jesus' conception, as both launch into prayers (or songs) of praise (1:41, 46–55). Zechariah is also filled with the Spirit to sing his prophetic worship song (vv. 67–79).

As we think about all these examples, a pattern emerges. In Luke 10, Jesus' Spirit-filled worship is a response to the disciples' successful mission trip and his vision of Satan falling from heaven (v. 18). Elizabeth and Mary are responding to the news of Jesus' conception and God's choice of the least over the greatest. Zechariah praises God for fulfilling his promise of a redeemer for Israel and for the birth of his own son, John, who will play a part in this redemption. We begin to see here that the Holy Spirit often inspires 'revelation' as well as 'response': people's praise is rooted in a fresh understanding or realization of the truths of God.

As leaders of worship, we need to think through the implications of this pattern. We might assume that creating a mood with a certain style of music or selection of songs will inspire worship in the Spirit, but (without downplaying the power or significance of appropriate music) the fact remains that there must be more to our worship than this. If Spirit-filled worship is a response to revelation, we need to make space for the truth of God to be freshly revealed to people, and think about whether we can facilitate this revelation.

 WORSHIP IDEAS

Consider again your use of Bible reading in worship. A carefully chosen passage, perhaps read over the top of instrumental music or projected on a screen with inspiring images as a background, can remind the congregation of God's truths. Allow space for the Holy Spirit to bring the passage to life and inspire people to worship in response to it.

Revelation can also come through sermons. How much thought do you give to songs or other forms of worship in response to the talk? Do you leave space for the Holy Spirit to apply the word to people's lives, perhaps with silence, instrumental music or a guided meditation—or do you simply rush into the next song on your list?

Often, testimony can be a really powerful means for the Holy Spirit to inspire people to worship. If you know people in your congregation with stories of God's faithfulness, why not invite them to share during a time of worship? Another way we have done this is to ask everyone in the congregation to write on a slip of paper one thing for which they want to give thanks to God. Then we have used a simple song like the chorus of Rich Mullins' 'Awesome God' and interspersed each chorus with readings from the slips of paper. This means that the worship is a genuine expression of what people are feeling, and it inspires people to glorify God in new ways.

ASKING FOR THE SPIRIT

Our daughter, Ella, was given a Christmas gift of a small mechanical cow. When you turned it on, it made an attempt at walking and let out a sound that was supposed to be a moo but actually sounded like a circular saw slicing wood. Unsurprisingly, Ella was petrified by it. At first we decided to use her fear to our advantage. Ella had developed a habit of crawling up to the bin and tipping out the contents, so, for a while, the cow stood guard in front of the bin and we had a clean floor. But after about twelve hours, Sara decided that we were being cruel parents, so she instigated a little reconciliation session where Ella got to touch the cow and discovered that she wasn't so scared after all.

A good gift, misunderstood, became an object of fear and a barrier for Ella. For too many Christians, the Holy Spirit is a bit like that. Some people are afraid or worried about him; perhaps they think he will cause uncontrolled or weird manifestations, or they might have been part of a church where so-called 'spiritual' occurrences were manipulative or insensitively handled. Other people might want to experience more of the Holy Spirit but feel that they are not in the élite spiritual 'club', one of those super-Christians who appear to have the Spirit on tap. For anyone who has ever felt any of those fears, these words from Jesus offer consolation.

'Which of you fathers, if your son asks for a fish, will give him a snake instead? Or if he asks for an egg, will give him a scorpion? If you then, though you are evil, know how to give good gifts to your children, how much more will your Father in heaven give the Holy Spirit to those who ask him!' (Luke 11:11–13).

The message is that our Father longs to give us his Holy Spirit, because he loves us as his children. If we are Christians, the Holy Spirit is already inside us, but if we are feeling dry and thirsty for more of him, Jesus promises that the Spirit will well up within us (John 7:37–39). He is not for the 'spiritually élite' (and anyone who sets themselves up as such is probably best avoided); he is for everyone, regardless of whether they have mystical experiences or supernatural feelings. The real test of being Spirit-filled is if we are empowered to live and worship more like Jesus (Galatians 5:22–25).

We see from Luke 11:5–10, immediately preceding the passage quoted above, that we need to keep asking, seeking and knocking at God's door for the Holy Spirit, like a friend persistently knocking on another friend's door in the middle of the night. We need to be filled and go on being filled. This is true for us as individuals and also corporately as we seek God to pour out more of his Spirit into our church worship. We should 'always pray and not give up' (18:1) for God to reveal more of himself.

For those who realize that they are actually afraid of the Holy Spirit, Luke 11 tells us that he is a 'good gift' from our loving heavenly Father (v. 13). He is not sent to harm us. We have personally found that the Holy Spirit is very polite and will only come into the parts of our lives where we invite him in. Our God is a God of order, not chaos (1 Corinthians 14:31–33). As leaders in the church, we should be careful to make space for the Holy Spirit, but also to be pastorally wise and sensitive about how services are run, so that everyone is brought along together and God's peace rules.

Sara grew up in a church that became increasingly charismatic as her teenage years progressed. While she remains grateful for all her experiences of the Holy Spirit from this time, from receiving the gift of tongues to the excitement that was termed 'the Toronto blessing', she became increasingly suspicious of some preachers' and worship leaders' apparent manipulation of 'spiritual gifts'. A service was deemed successful only if there had been physical manifestations of the Spirit, and speaking in tongues was more important than conversion. By the time she arrived at Bible college, she was ready to embrace scepticism towards charismatic worship and sink into a comfortable ambivalence towards the Holy Spirit.

It was a few years into our time at our previous church, Ascension, when Sara started feeling confident and safe enough to start exploring again the whole area of ministry in the power of the Spirit. The church inspired confidence in her because of a wise approach towards the gifts of the Spirit, with clear pastoral guidelines for service and worship leaders. As we describe them, you may want to consider whether similar guidelines might be useful in your context (if you don't already have them).

We often left space for the Holy Spirit to speak and minister in services, and sometimes this would lead to more obvious physical manifestations for some people, such as shaking, falling or crying out. Whenever this happened, the person leading the service would always calmly explain to the congregation what was going on. It was the leader's responsibility to discern whether to pause and allow more time for engaging with God, or to move on to prevent over-emotionalism or hype.

A trained prayer ministry team, overseen by an experienced team leader, was available to pray with people at every service. If this led to a more unusual reaction in a person, the team knew how to continue praying with that person and, if necessary, bring to an end any unhelpful or attention-seeking behaviour. We also made space on many occasions for people to receive prayer for healing, either as a result of a word of knowledge or simply because they had a need. We saw some miraculous healings but also recognized the need to deal pastorally with those who didn't receive an immediate response.

Most of our times of receiving words of prophecy for the church were done as a team. Before each worship service, we would ask God to speak specifically with regard to anything he wanted to do in the service. We would listen in silence together and then share our impressions. The benefit of doing this as a group was the space created for confirmation and accountability: when a word is repeated several times, you can have more confidence that it is from God, and it can be used in a service with integrity.

If someone had a word of prophecy during a service, we would ask them to share it with a church leader and/or the service leader before it was considered for broadcast to the entire congregation. In this way, words that were potentially unhelpful in pastoral terms or actually in opposition to the church's values could be tested rather than let loose to cause havoc and hurt in the church.

These guidelines are not suggested as a way of stifling the Spirit: he blows wherever he pleases (John 3:8)! They are just ways that our church found to be helpful in steering clear of chaotic or insensitive times of ministry, which might have very little to do with the 'good gift' that our Father loves to give us.

THE SECRET PLACE OF PRAYER

'The news about him spread all the more, so that crowds of people came to hear him and to be healed of their sicknesses. But Jesus often withdrew to lonely places and prayed' (Luke 5:15–16).

When you read through Luke's Gospel, it is remarkable how many times you see Jesus withdrawing for times of prayer with his Father. When pressure is mounting, it seems that Jesus' need for solitude becomes all the more important. This passage shows that the more success he has in ministry, the more he pulls back to reconnect with his Father. Luke 9:10 tells how Jesus modelled this with his disciples by withdrawing with them after an intense time of ministry. Perhaps the key to Jesus' perfect reliance on the Spirit can be found in these times spent in the secret place of prayer.

In Luke 4:38–44 we read the description of a fairly stressful sabbath in Jesus' life. It starts with teaching and driving out a demon in the synagogue, continues with the healing of Peter's mother-in-law, and, as the day draws to a close, the entire town bring their sick people to Jesus for healing. Where a good night's sleep would be in order for most of us at this point, Jesus leaves to go to a solitary place (and, in the parallel passage in Mark 1:35, we learn that his purpose is prayer). What is said between Jesus and the Father at this point? We don't know, but somehow he must have had a renewed sense of his identity and calling because, in the following verses, we witness the clarity with which he makes a decision to move on, despite people begging him to stay, 'because that is why I was sent' (Luke 4:43).

One of the big lessons we have learnt during our (relatively short) time in ministry is that, as leaders in the church, we cannot rely on church services as our main 'time with God'. Members of the congregation may find Sunday a time of sabbath rest, when they get spiritual input and space to reflect, but, if you are heavily involved in your church as a volunteer or staff member, you have probably noticed that this doesn't quite work for you. Of course, in serving our congregations we are offering pleasing worship to God, and there may be moments when we can personally connect with him. In general, though, when you are thinking about the PA system or the right chords, or discerning the pastoral needs of the congregation, you are perhaps not in the best place to rest in God's presence.

It seems that Jesus had similar experiences, so he set up a pattern of withdrawing to spend time alone with the Father, to be refreshed by him through the Holy Spirit. Often, we think we can somehow fit God in while prioritizing everything else before him: he gets snatched moments between activities, or sleepy prayers as we wake up or fall asleep. What happens when we treat our friends or spouses like this? They get fed up fairly quickly. Quality relationships need quality time devoted to them, and the only way to do that is to put time with that person in the diary as a priority.

Spending proper sabbath time with God, alone with him in the secret place of prayer, means that we get the chance to reconnect with our identity as worship leaders. We remember our calling and the challenge to be a humble servant. We can offer unrestrained worship with our voices and instruments or through other artistic expressions. We can bring to God our frustrations, disappointments and failures. We can read and be refreshed by his word or devotional books, or by listening to sermon recordings or inspiring music. We can rest in the presence of his Holy Spirit, knowing the acceptance of our loving Father, which does not come from our ministry or accomplishments but from our identity in Christ as a son or daughter of the king.

We suggest that you get out your diary right now and plan in some intentional sabbath time, just you and God, over the next few months. It might be half an hour, half a day or a couple of days where you go away on retreat, perhaps starting with a short amount of time and building up. What is important, though, is finding a place where you are not disturbed in any way. Set up for yourself some kind of pattern of prayer and retreat, where you can worship God with no other agenda than his worthiness. You will find that these times in the secret place will be like oases of refreshing water for your life of worship and your ministry of worship leading.

⁜

CONCLUSION

As we come to the end of this journey of exploring how Jesus leads and inspires us to lead worship, how are you feeling? Challenged? Encouraged? Overwhelmed? There can often be a pressure after reading a book, returning from a big conference or visiting another church, to 'do it like they do'. We can assume that if we sing the same songs, or use the same instruments, or buy the same technology, somehow we will capture the kind of worship 'they' have. But that is not the purpose of this book. We want to help you explore principles and values from our understanding of Jesus, but our heart's desire is that you express these values in ways that reflect your church community and the people you are trying to reach.

We can have confidence that if our worship is inspired by Jesus, and offered in Christ to the Father by the Spirit, the shape and style of how we do it can take a million forms. As Ron Man puts it, 'There is no one right style or form for worship. Jesus Christ our worship leader has taken innumerable forms of worship across the centuries and across the world and made them his own.'[1]

We need to take the pressure off ourselves: we don't have to be like anyone else. We shouldn't be competing with any other worship leader, and we certainly don't need to impress God. Because of Jesus, our worship is perfect, and by the Spirit we can draw near to the Father, who loves it when we worship him.

 WORSHIP EXPERIENCE

We want to close by focusing on a wonderful hymn by Fanny Crosby (1820–1915). This remarkable woman was possibly the most prolific hymn writer in history, writing over 8000 hymns, despite being blind from the age of six. 'To God be the glory' may be so well known to you that you find it easy to miss the depth and beauty of her lyrics, as they are a reminder of what worship is all about—drawing near to the Father through Jesus the Son, to give him alone all the glory.

Read through the lyrics, reflect and allow God to speak to you through them. You might want to use them as an inspiration for your own expression of worship. Write a new tune to them, paraphrase them in your own words, paint or draw them, dance them, make a creative video or PowerPoint presentation using them, cross-stitch them on to a pillow case... let your creativity run wild!

To God be the glory, great things He has done;
so loved He the world that He gave us His Son,
who yielded His life an atonement for sin,
and opened the life gate that all may go in.

Praise the Lord, praise the Lord,
let the earth hear His voice!
Praise the Lord, praise the Lord,
let the people rejoice!
O come to the Father, through Jesus the Son,
and give Him the glory, great things He has done.

O perfect redemption, the purchase of blood,
to every believer the promise of God;
the vilest offender who truly believes,
that moment from Jesus a pardon receives.

Great things He has taught us, great things He has done,
and great our rejoicing through Jesus the Son;
but purer, and higher, and greater will be
our wonder, our worship, when Jesus we see.

PLANNING A SERVICE

This section sets out to answer the question 'How do you plan a worship time?' It may look a little complicated at first glance, and certainly, the more experience you gain in planning services, the more intuitive it can become. But if you have never prepared in this way before, you might find it helpful to follow this structure or adapt it to your context, and soon you will find it coming naturally.

Sermon/service theme(s):		
Bible reading(s):		
Congregation:		
Type of service:		
Structure	**What you are trying to achieve**	**Songs/activities**

As you can see, what we consider first is the theme(s) of the service. In doing this, we are acknowledging the authority of the preacher and the wider team or individuals who devise the sermon and service plans. We might be leading on a week when the preacher is talking about Jesus washing the disciples' feet, or it might be Harvest Sunday, or the church could be starting a new series on Jesus in the workplace. This is not to say that all the songs have to centre on the theme: this can become a very tiresome way of leading worship. It is just good to know the overall context and somehow reflect and respond to it in worship.

Then we read through any Bible passages for that Sunday. Your church might follow the lectionary or be preaching through a book of the Bible, or someone might choose one or more passage depending on their topic. As you read, reflect on how you might interact with the passage in worship, and consider whether there are any creative ways in which you might be able to bring the passage to life for your congregation.

Next, find out the nature of the congregation, the type of service, and any other key elements. It is worth knowing, for instance, how much time is available for sung worship, whether children will be present throughout, if it is a baptism with lots of visitors who may or may not be familiar with church, if a missionary is coming to do a presentation, if it is a Communion service, and so on.

Of course, yours may be a church in which finding out the preacher's topic is very difficult until late on Saturday night (or early Sunday morning). In this case you can only go with what you are given. If you want to take the planning process seriously, however, it may be worth having a polite conversation with your pastor, service leaders or preaching team, explaining how helpful it would be to receive information about themes and service content as early as possible.

All being well, the themes, Bible verses and structure will be triggering off some songs or other worship ideas in your head. Note them down. But the next stage is to stop, pray and listen. Ask God to put in your mind scriptures, pictures, songs or worship ideas. You may feel inexperienced at this, but remember that we can all hear God—although it may be simply through a thought or an impression rather than choirs of angels writing messages on the wall! God usually wants to speak to us more than we want to stop and listen.

Now test these thoughts against scripture. For example, an image of you leading worship naked is probably not from God: it will not encourage people to worship 'in a fitting and orderly way' (1 Corinthians 14:40)! Also, test your thoughts against the theme and service order. If you think that worship should be an open-ended praise-fest this week, in which you might not even find time for the sermon, does that fit in with the ten minutes you have actually been given between the notices and the Boys' Brigade presentation?

By this stage, you should be able to start working out a flow of movements of worship—what you are aiming to do in your worship time. In Chapter 3 we gave examples of what these could be, based on the Psalms. Remember, your goal is to take people on a worship journey, progressing from one movement to the next in a logical way.

Once you have this kind of structure, it is simply a matter of deciding which songs or other modes of worship best achieve your aims. While we have talked about exploring creative methods of worship other than singing, for now we will focus, for simplicity's sake, on song choices.

The main criterion is whether the songs fulfil the worship objectives, but a few other things to consider are follows.

- Does the congregation know the song? You don't want to introduce more than one new song in a service, unless it is very easy to pick up. Is it singable by this particular congregation and playable by the musicians?
- Does it fit into the flow of worship? The songs do not all have to be in the same key and tempo, yet there should be some sort of natural progression from one to the next.
- Is there a mixture of 'content' songs and 'response' songs? A content song might be a hymn or a contemporary song that reveals something of God in its lyrics. A 'response' song will focus more on what we are moved to do as a result. Some songs do both, to a greater or lesser degree, and sometimes you might want to lean towards one type of song for a specific purpose, but it is generally important to keep them in balance.

- Is there a balance of personal songs ('I') and corporate songs ('We')?

On the following pages are two real-life examples to demonstrate how your planning sheet might look when completed, with suggestions of songs and activities. We wouldn't suggest attempting all these activities in one service—two or three at the most will be fine. Don't forget, these are just samples from our context, and yours might look very different.

EXAMPLE 1

Sermon theme:	The footwashing king	
Bible reading:	John 13:1–17	
Congregation:	Mix of ages. Children out after notices	
Type of service:	Informal morning worship	
Structure	**Aims/movement of worship**	**Ideas for songs/activities**
Opening worship	Gather people, focus them on God	Come all you people,[1] We've come to praise you,[2] Drawing near.[3]
Welcome		
Worship time (15 mins)	Engage children and adults	*Song:* Words are not enough.[4] *Activities:* Get everyone to write one name of God on a piece of paper and fold it to make a paper plane. Throw them together, then read each other's out as an act of spoken praise.
	Express Jesus' majesty, to contrast his humility, which will be highlighted in the sermon.	*Songs:* Crown him with many crowns,[5] You are God (Glorious).[6] *Activities:* Have props of a crown, a throne and a robe. Get people to imagine how they'd feel if the Queen came to the service, and how much more we should honour King Jesus.
	End by reflecting on his coming as a human to serve.	*Songs:* Light of the world,[7] Who is this?[8] *Activities:* Swap the kingly clothes for simple sandals, stick and a crown of thorns.
Notices, children out		Do the notices as a quiz, with small prizes for the right answers.
Bible reading	John 13:1–17	Have one narrator and two dancers or actors to dance or mime the parts of Jesus and Peter.
Sermon	The footwashing king	
Response time	Focus on humility, our following in Jesus' example.	*Songs:* Humble King,[9] From heaven you came (Servant King),[10] What kind of throne.[11] *Activities:* Washing each other's feet.
Closing prayer	Commitment to go out with humility and service.	Use John Wesley's Covenant Prayer.
Final song	Send people out to serve others.	All I have.[12]

EXAMPLE 2

Sermon theme:	God @ work	
Bible readings:	Daniel 1:1–21; Colossians 3:23–24	
Congregation:	Adult	
Type of service:	Evening worship	
Structure	**Aims/movement of worship**	**Ideas for songs/activities**
Welcome	Service leader to introduce theme.	Use video of church members walking to their different places of work.
Worship time	Opportunity for people to bring their burdens from the week and give them to God, and receive his Holy Spirit.	Songs: Veni Sancte Spiritus,[13] All who are thirsty.[14] Activities: Hands clenched: people remember their stresses and worries. Slowly open hands to release worries to God and receive his Spirit.
	Reminder of God's faithfulness in our work situations.	Activities: Testimonies from different people about how God has been present or helped them to witness at work. Songs: Great is your faithfulness,[15] I lift my eyes to the hills.[16]
Bible reading	Daniel 1	Read dramatically, with one person as narrator and another speaking the other characters.
Worship time	Asking God to speak through his word	Speak, O Lord.[17]
Sermon	God @ work	Make use of the Christian Life and Work DVD,[18] or Mark Greene's books Thank God It's Monday or Supporting Christians at Work.[19]
Response time	Prayer for those in work	Activities: ask those who have jobs outside the church to stand and be prayed for. Anoint with oil. Or get people into small groups to pray for each other's work (be sensitive towards those who may be unemployed).
Worship time	Asking God to empower to be his salt and light in our situation.	Songs: Breathe on me, breath of God.[20] Repeat the first line of the carol O come, O come, Immanuel as an introduction to Great is the darkness.[21]
Closing prayer	Sending out prayer	Activities: Give out small sachets of salt and single matches, as a reminder to be salt and light in our workplaces.

✣

Appendix 2

SAMPLE LITURGY

The following liturgy, written by Ruth Neve for the 2008 Baptist Assembly alternative venue 'Prism', is included with permission for use in church services. You may photocopy these pages or download the text from the link at www.brf.org.uk/9781841016153 for non-profit purposes. Unless otherwise indicated, Bible verses are quoted from or based on the New Living Translation.

The leader speaks the regular text, the congregation the bold text. Instructions are in italics. The mood is of joy and celebration and, if possible, the table should be placed in the centre of the room, with a lavish amount of bread and wine and grape juice to symbolize a feast.

COVENANT FEAST: A BANQUET OF HOPE

Gathering liturgy

We gather to celebrate a covenant feast at the invitation of Almighty God.

We join with those who have gone before and with those who will follow.

We celebrate with Israel's leaders as they share a covenant meal with God at Sinai.

We celebrate with the disciples as they share the Passover feast, break bread and drink wine, symbolizing the new covenant between God and his people.

We celebrate with all peoples and all nations as we partake in

Reproduced with permission from How Would Jesus Lead Worship? *by Sam and Sara Hargreaves (BRF, 2009), ISBN 978 1 84101 615 3*

the wonderful feast that God spreads to celebrate the salvation he brings—on the day that death dies and God wipes away all tears.

These covenant feasts are a time of joy and celebration—of singing, of bounty and of nourishment—bringing honour and praise to God.

People of the covenant, let us join together and praise God for his wonderful deeds and perfect faithfulness.

'O Lord, we will honour and praise your name, for you are our God. You do such wonderful things.' *(Isaiah 25:1)*

Songs of joy and celebration

Do this in remembrance of me

'In that day the people will proclaim—

"This is our God. We trusted in him, and he saved us. This is the Lord, in whom we trusted. Let us rejoice in the salvation he brings!"' *(Isaiah 25:9)*

Each person brings their own testimony of God's trustworthiness, his salvation and goodness to the feast. Break up into 3s or 4s and share together your testimony of God's faithfulness.

Regathering song about trustworthiness/faithfulness of God

Symbolic act

Reader 1: 'In that day he will remove the cloud of gloom, the shadow of death that hangs over the earth. He will swallow up death forever!' *(Isaiah 25:7–8)*

Reproduced with permission from How Would Jesus Lead Worship? *by Sam and Sara Hargreaves (BRF, 2009), ISBN 978 1 84101 615 3*

Reader 2: 'Then Jesus uttered another loud cry and breathed his last. And the curtain in the sanctuary of the Temple was torn in two, from top to bottom. When the Roman officer who stood facing him saw how he had died, he exclaimed, "Truly, this was the Son of God!"' (*Mark 15:37–39*)

Have two people holding a black cloth on the stage or over the congregation, and then tear it in two.

Song celebrating end of death/resurrection

Invitation to feast

You have come to Mount Zion, to the city of the living God, the heavenly Jerusalem, and to countless thousands of angels in joyful assembly.

We have come to the covenant feast.

You have come to the assembly of God's firstborn children, whose names are written in heaven.

We have come to the covenant feast.

You have come to God himself, who is the judge of all people.

We have come to the covenant feast.

You have come to Jesus, whose sprinkled blood of forgiveness mediates the new covenant between God and people. (*Hebrews 12:22–24*)

We have come to the covenant feast.

Reproduced with permission from How Would Jesus Lead Worship? *by Sam and Sara Hargreaves (BRF, 2009), ISBN 978 1 84101 615 3*

'Jesus took a loaf of bread, asked God's blessing on it and broke it saying, "Take it, for this is my body." Jesus took a cup of wine and gave thanks to God for it and said, "This is my blood, poured out for many, sealing the covenant between God and his people."' *(Based on Mark 14:22–24)*

'This is our God. We trusted in him, and he saved us. This is the Lord, in whom we trusted. Let us rejoice in the salvation he brings!' *(Isaiah 25:9)*

Covenant feast

Take bread and, asking for God's blessing, share it with one another.

Take a cup of wine or juice and, in thankfulness to God, share together in the feast of the covenant.

(Joyful/dance music as sound backdrop)

Time for reflective prayers of intercession

This day has not yet come.

'For the poor, God is a refuge from the storm. For the needy in distress, you are a shelter from the rain and heat. You silence the roar of oppressive nations, you cool the land with the shade of a cloud.' *(Based on Isaiah 25:4–5)*

Pray that the poor and oppressed will know this reality breaking in now.

Reproduced with permission from How Would Jesus Lead Worship? *by Sam and Sara Hargreaves (BRF, 2009), ISBN 978 1 84101 615 3*

Time for prayer/reflection on images of current situations in silence. Say or sing, 'Through our lives and by our prayers, your Kingdom come'[1] at a number of intervals.

Closing liturgy

'The Lord Almighty will spread a wonderful feast for everyone around the world. It will be a delicious feast of good food, with clear, well-aged wine and choice beef. In that day he will remove the cloud of gloom, the shadow of death that hangs over the earth. He will swallow up death forever! The Sovereign Lord will wipe away all tears. He will remove for ever the insults and mockery against his land and people. The Lord has spoken!' *(Isaiah 25:6–8)*

All: Amen! Come, Lord Jesus!

Final celebratory song

© RUTH NEVE 2008

✠

BIBLIOGRAPHY

THEOLOGY OF WORSHIP

Armstrong, John H. (ed.), *Reformation and Revival: Restoring True Worship Pt 1* (Reformation and Revival, 2000)

Cocksworth, Christopher, *Holy, Holy, Holy* (DLT, 1997)

Kauflin, Bob, *Worship Matters* (Crossway, 2008)

Man, Ron, *Proclamation and Praise* (Wipf and Stock, 2007)

Parry, Robin, *Worshipping Trinity* (Paternoster Press, 2005)

Peterson, David, *Engaging with God* (Apollos, 1992)

Torrance, James B., *Worship, Community and the Triune God of Grace* (Paternoster Press, 1996)

THE TRINITY

Jenson, Robert, *The Triune Identity* (Fortress Press, 1982)

McFarlane, Graham, *Why Do You Believe What You Believe about the Holy Spirit?* (Paternoster Press, 1998)

LUKE

Green, Joel, *New International Commentary on the New Testament: Luke* (Eerdmans, 1997)

Johnson, Luke Timothy, *The Gospel of Luke* (Liturgical Press, 1991)

Marshall, I. Howard, *New International Greek Testament Commentary: Luke* (Paternoster Press, 1978)

Morris, Leon, *Tyndale New Testament Commentaries: Luke* (IVP, 1988)

Wilcock, Michael, *The Bible Speaks Today: The Message of Luke* (IVP, 1979)

Wright, Tom, *Luke for Everyone* (SPCK, 2001)

OTHER BIBLE COMMENTARIES

Bruce, F.F., *New London Commentary on the New Testament: Hebrews* (Marshall, Morgan and Scott, 1964)

France, R.T., *New International Greek Testament Commentary: Mark* (Eerdmans, 2002)

WORSHIP, ART AND CREATIVITY

Baker, Jonny and Gay, Doug, *Alternative Worship* (Baker, 2004)

Beach, Nancy, *An Hour on Sunday* (Zondervan, 2004)

Bell, John L., *The Singing Thing* (Wild Goose Publications, 2000)

Bell, John L., *The Singing Thing Too* (Wild Goose Publications, 2007)

Dryness, William A., *Visual Faith* (Baker Academic, 2001)

Flannagan, Andy, *Distinctive Worship* (Spring Harvest, 2005)

Kelly, Gerard, *Spoken Worship* (Zondervan, 2007)

Lacey, Rob, *Are We Getting Through?* (Silver Fish, 1999)

Liesch, Barry, *The New Worship* (Baker, 2001)

Nichols, Aidan, *The Art of God Incarnate* (DLT, 1980)

Shaeffer, Francis A., *Art and the Bible* (L'Abri Fellowship, 1973)

Turner, Steve, *Imagine* (IVP, 2001)

Wallace, Sue, *Multi-Sensory Prayer* (SU, 2000)

Wallace, Sue, *Multi-Sensory Church* (SU, 2002)

Wallace, Sue, *Multi-Sensory Scripture* (SU, 2005)

Ward, Pete (ed.), *Mass Culture* (BRF, 1999, 2008)

SONG BOOKS

Come All You People (Wild Goose Resource Group, 1994)

Heaven Shall Not Wait (Wild Goose Resource Group, 1989)

Love from Below (Wild Goose Resource Group, 1989)

Sing Glory (Kevin Mayhew, 2000)

Spring Harvest Praise 2002

Spring Harvest Praise 08/09

World Praise 2 (Church Street Press, 1999)

Worship Today (Spring Harvest, 2001)

LEADERSHIP

Hybels, Bill, *Courageous Leadership* (Zondervan, 2002)

Lawrence, James, *Growing Leaders* (BRF, 2004)

✛

NOTES

Introduction to Part 1

1 Examples taken from Christopher Cocksworth, *Holy, Holy, Holy* (DLT, 1997), p. 61. The best survey of the New Testament words for worship can be found in David Peterson, *Engaging with God* (Apollos, 1992), pp. 55–74.

2 Matt Redman, 'The heart of worship', copyright © 1997 Thankyou Music. Adm. by worshiptogether.com songs excl. UK & Europe, adm. by kingswaysongs.com tym@kingsway.co.uk.

3 London School of Theology was then known as London Bible College. Check out www.lst.ac.uk for more information on the course.

4 You can read an article version of this paper on www.samandsara.net/resources/jesus_is_my_girlfriend.pdf, originally published on the now defunct www.heartofworship.com

5 Email interview, received 7 May 2001.

6 James B. Torrance, *Worship, Community and the Triune God of Grace* (Paternoster Press, 1996), p. ix.

7 For example, this simple song is a three-part round, so it involves people in trinitarian worship both through the lyrics and symbolically through the music.
Jesus lead us to the Father, help us draw near.
As we come with awe and gladness, help us draw near.
Alleluia, alleluia, help us draw near.
© Sam Hargreaves / RESOUNDworship.org, Administered by The Jubilate Group, 4 Thorne Park Road, Torquay TQ2 6RX, UK copyrightmanager@jubilate.co.uk. MP3 and sheet music available for free at www.RESOUNDworship.org.

8 For an excellent survey of tensions in worship leading, see Bob Kauflin, *Worship Matters* (Crossway, 2008).

Chapter 1: Jesus is my worship leader?

1 Torrance, *Worship*, pp. 47, 53–54.

2 For a thorough look at Jesus as worship leader in Hebrews 2:12, see Ron Man, *Proclamation and Praise* (Wipf and Stock, 2007).

3 See Peterson, *Engaging with God*, Chapter 1, for an overview of the Old Testament sacrificial system as worship.

4   There were people who served as temple music leaders: see 1 Chronicles 6:31–32 and 2 Chronicles 5:12–13 for examples. These can offer us some insight into a church musician's role but they were not fundamentally the leaders of worship.

5   You could think of the climactic scene in *Raiders of the Lost Ark* (Dir. Steven Spielberg, 1981), where the ark of the covenant is opened by the Nazis, and the glory of God dramatically obliterates them.

6   F.F. Bruce, *New London Commentary on the New Testament: Hebrews* (Marshall, Morgan and Scott Ltd, 1964), p. 246.

7   Ron Man, 'Jesus our Worship Leader' in John H. Armstrong (ed.), *Reformation and Revival: Restoring True Worship Pt 1* (Reformation and Revival, 2000), p. 33.

8   *Jesus, you know what it's like to be human, took off your glory, entered our story.*
    Jesus, you know what it's like to be me, so I'll trust you, completely, utterly.
    Jesus, you know what it's like to be lonely, tired and hungry, excited and clumsy.
    Jesus, you know what it's like to be me, so I'll trust you, completely, utterly.
    Jesus you know what it's like to be tempted. Yet you were faithful, loving and grace-filled.
    I want to see all those things here in me, so I'll trust you, completely, utterly.
    © Sam Hargreaves

9   We will delve deeper into examples of this in Chapter 5, and its implications for how we lead worship.

10 We obviously don't have room here to explore this subject as much as we would like. A very readable introduction to the Trinity in reference to worship is Robin Parry, *Worshipping Trinity* (Paternoster Press, 2005). For something a bit more weighty, try Cocksworth, *Holy, Holy, Holy.*

11 Robert Jenson, *The Triune Identity* (Fortress Press, 1982), p. xii.

12 Cocksworth, *Holy, Holy, Holy*, p. 33.

13 We don't have space here to discuss whether or in what way we should worship the Holy Spirit directly. There are no biblical references to worshipping the Spirit (for a fuller argument, see Graham McFarlane, *Why Do You Believe What You Believe about the Holy Spirit,* Paternoster Press, 1998), and yet the creeds say of the Spirit that 'with the Father and the Son he is worshipped and glorified'. (For the other side of the argument, see Parry, *Worshipping Trinity*, pp. 112–114.)

14 Words by Charitie Lees Bancroft, tune by Vikki Cook, © 1993 PDI Worship, available in *Worship Today* (Spring Harvest)

15 For instance, 'Sing glory to God the Father', Michael Saward, © Michael Saward/ Jubilate Group, available in the book *Sing Glory* and on www.jubilate.co.uk.

16 For instance, 'Father God I wonder', Ian Smale, © 1984 Thankyou Music; 'Father let me dedicate', verses Lawrence Tuttiet (1825–97)/Adpt. Matt Redman, chorus by Louie Giglio, Jesse Reeves and Chris Tomlin, © 2003 Thankyou Music/ worshiptogether.com; both available on www.kingswaysongs.com

17 For instance, 'First in pouring out your love', Geraldine Latty, © 2004 Thankyou Music; available on www.kingswaysongs.com. 'Who is this?' © Joel

Payne/RESOUNDworship.org admin by Jubilate Group; available on www. RESOUNDworship.org

18 For instance, 'Come, Holy Spirit', John L. Bell, © 1995 WGRG, Iona Community, available in the book *Come All You People* from www.ionabooks.com; 'There must be more than this', Tim Hughes, © 2002 Thankyou Music, available on www. kingswaysongs.com

Introduction to Part 2

1 Dir. James Mangold, 2005.
2 Published by Thomas Nelson, 2004.
3 See Leon Morris, *Tyndale New Testament Commentaries: Luke* (IVP, 1988), pp. 44–45.

Chapter 2: Humble servant

1 I. Howard Marshall, *New International Greek Testament Commentary, Luke* (Paternoster Press, 1978), p. 166.
2 Joel Green, *New International Commentary on the New Testament: Luke* (Eerdmans, 1997), p. 192.
3 Marshall, *Luke,* p. 172.
4 Morris, *Luke,* p. 185.
5 Morris, *Luke,* p. 186.
6 Both of these are available on iTunes; note that not all of the Wainwright album is quite so sanctified!
7 © 1995 IQ Music Limited.
8 *Sing Glory: Hymns, Psalms and Songs for a New Century* (Kevin Mayhew, 2000).
9 Morris, *Luke,* p. 193.
10 For excellent resources and training for worship with children see Big Ministries website, www.bigministries.co.uk, and www.familyworship.org.uk
11 For resources for worship with people who have learning disabilities see Causeway Prospects website: www.prospects.org.uk
12 Michael Wilcock, *The Bible Speaks Today: The Message of Luke* (IVP, 1979), p. 114.
13 Marshall, *Luke,* p. 181.
14 Jesus accepted children (Luke 9:48; 18:16) and women (8:1–3), neither group having much standing in that culture. When Martha suggested that Mary should take the place expected of her by society—back in the kitchen—Jesus responded that she had done right by daring to enter a traditional man's world and spend time with him (10:38–42) (Tom Wright, *Luke for Everyone,* SPCK, 2001, p. 130). He accepted the embarrassing people, such as a blind man shouting at him, whom others told to shut up (18:35–43). He accepted 'sinners': Zacchaeus, a despised

tax collector (19:1–10), a prostitute at the home of a prominent Pharisee (7:36–50), and other 'outcasts' (15:1–2). He showed compassion to a demon-possessed man (8:26–39), he risked becoming ceremonially unclean by touching the dead (7:11–17), he allowed sick people to touch him (8:43–48) and broke the sabbath rules because of his concern to heal (13:10–17).

15 Baptist World Alliance, July 2005

16 Spring Harvest Praise 08/09, www.andyflan.com

17 For resources to help you engage with slavery and trafficking issues, visit www.stopthetraffik.org and www.antislaveryinternational.org.uk

18 The 24-7 prayer website is very useful for facts and stories, and has an online version of Operation World for information about praying for all the countries of the world. www.24-7prayer.com

19 Again, both of these tracks are available to download from iTunes.

20 www.tearfund.org, youth.tearfund.org, www.christian-aid.org.uk

21 © 1989 WGRG, Iona Community, Glasgow G2 3DH, Scotland. Available in the book *Love From Below,* published by Wild Goose: see www.ionabooks.com

22 © Andy Flannagan, mp3s and chord charts available for free at www.andyflan.com/organicworship, full sheet music in Spring Harvest 08/09.

23 © Kingsway's Thankyou music, available on www.kingswaysongs.com

24 © Kingsway's Thankyou music, available on www.kingswaysongs.com

Chapter 3: Leader with authority

1 Our favourite leadership book is Bill Hybels, *Courageous Leadership* (Zondervan, 2002).

2 In Mark 6:6 he marvels at his home town's unbelief, but that is not quite the same...

3 Marshall, *Luke*, p. 433.

4 Marshall, *Luke*, p. 352.

5 Marshall, *Luke*, p. 353.

6 Morris, *Luke*, p. 337.

Chapter 4: Creative communicator

1 The pub down the road was called the Sylvan Moon, so this was supposed to 'eclipse' a trip to the Moon...

2 Marshall, *Luke*, p. 561.

3 Morris, *Luke*, p. 246.

4 Two books we have found very helpful in thinking through different types of worship have been Nancy Beach (former creative director of Willow Creek Community Church), *An Hour on Sunday* (Zondervan, 2004), and Andy Flannagan, *Distinctive*

Worship (Spring Harvest, 2005), which is supposed to be about youth but has many applications for wider church worship.

5 Two great books on a theology of art are Steve Turner, Imagine (IVP, 2001), and Francis A. Schaeffer, Art and the Bible (L'Abri Fellowship, 1973).

6 Aidan Nichols, The Art of God Incarnate (DLT, 1980), p. 50.

7 William A. Dryness, Visual Faith (Baker Academic, 2001), p. 144.

8 For a very practical look on the importance of helping people to sing, read John L. Bell, The Singing Thing (Wild Goose Publications, 2000), and The Singing Thing Too (Wild Goose Publications, 2007).

9 Marshall, Luke, p. 304.

10 For more ideas, see the series of books by Sue Wallace (leader of the creative service Visions in York, www.visions-york.org), Multi-Sensory Prayer, Multi-Sensory Church and Multi-Sensory Scripture, all Scripture Union. A growing, searchable archive of creative worship ideas can be found at www.engageworship.org.

11 John Barnett, © 1988 Mercy/Vineyard.

12 Makoto Fujimura is an inspirational Christian artist working in New York. His website www.makotofujimura.com has many great articles, including an excellent 'Ten Commandments for Artists'. www.veritasse.co.uk offers a community for UK Christian artists, and you can be inspired by their work.

13 We often use tracks from Ma Fleur by Cinematic Orchestra (Ninja Tune, 2007), Seven Days of Falling by Esbjörn Svensson Trio (Superstudio GUL, 2003), and the piano music of Eric Satie.

14 Two great books on this are Rob Lacey, Are We Getting Through? (Silver Fish, 1999), and Gerard Kelly, Spoken Worship (Zondervan, 2007).

15 R.T. France, New International Greek Testament Commentary: Mark (Eerdmans, 2002), pp. 198–199.

16 Interestingly, he uses the same metaphor in Matthew 5:14–16 but with a different message.

17 The quotation from Isaiah is not proclaiming God's intention for Isaiah or Jesus' listeners, as if he doesn't want them to hear. It is rather the sad, inevitable outcome of speaking the truth in a fallen world. The words are spoken with bitter irony, as brought out in B. Hollenbach's translation: '... so that they may indeed see but not perceive, and may indeed hear but not understand; because the last thing they want is to turn and have their sins forgiven!' as quoted in France, Mark, p. 200.

18 Marshall, Luke, p. 323.

19 France, Mark, p. 183.

20 Wright, Luke for Everyone, p. 95.

21 For an excellent look at Communion from a number of leading worship thinkers, see Pete Ward (ed.), Mass Culture (BRF, 1999, revised and expanded 2008).

22 Paul speaks of Jesus as the Passover lamb in 1 Corinthians 5:7–8.

23 Green, Luke, p. 758.

24 Torrance, Worship, pp. 10–11.

25 Dir. Roland Joffé, 1986.
26 For Celtic worship resources, visit www.northumbriacommunity.org and www. faithandworship.com.
27 See the book *World Praise 2* (Church Street Press, 1999).
28 Although this stream has influenced us greatly, and we recommend Jonny Baker and Doug Gay, *Alternative Worship* (Baker, 2004), as well as jonnybaker.blogs.com and alternativeworship.org.

Chapter 5: Reliant on the Spirit

1 Luke Timothy Johnson, *The Gospel of Luke* (Liturgical Press, 1991), p. 91.
2 Wright, *Luke for Everyone,* p. 123.
3 Johnson, *The Gospel of Luke*, p. 169.

Conclusion

1 Man, 'Jesus our Worship Leader', p. 38.

Appendix 1: Planning a service

1 John L. Bell © Iona Community, available in the book *Come All You People* (www. ionabooks.com).
2 Kate Simmonds and Stuart Townend, © Thankyou Music, available on www. kingswaysongs.com
3 Sam Hargreaves © Sam Hargreaves/RESOUNDworship.org admin by Jubilate Group, available free on www.RESOUNDworship.org
4 Damian Herbert, © Big Ministries, available in *Spring Harvest Kids Praise Party Vol 2.*
5 Matthew Bridges (1800–1894) and Godfrey Thring (1823–1903), available in the book *Worship Today* (Spring Harvest).
6 Matt Osgood © Matt Osgood/RESOUNDworship.org admin by Jubilate Group, available for free on www.RESOUNDworship.org
7 Tim Hughes, © Thankyou Music, available on www.kingswaysongs.com.
8 Joel Payne, © Joel Payne/RESOUNDworship.org admin by Jubilate Group, available free on www.RESOUNDworship.org.
9 Brenton Brown © Vineyard Songs, available in the book *Spring Harvest Praise 2003.*
10 Graham Kendrick © Make Way Music, available in the book *Worship Today* (Spring Harvest).
11 Joel Payne, © Joel Payne/RESOUNDworship.org admin by Jubilate Group, available free on www.RESOUNDworship.org.

12 Matt Osgood © Matt Osgood/RESOUNDworship.org admin by Jubilate Group, available free on www.RESOUNDworship.org.

13 Jaques Berthier, © Taize Community, available free on www.taize.fr.

14 Brenton Brown and Glenn Robertson, © Vineyard Songs, available in the book *Spring Harvest Praise 2002*.

15 Thomas Chisholm (1866–1960), available in the book *Worship Today* (Spring Harvest).

16 Judy Gresham, © Judy Gresham/RESOUNDworship.org admin by the Jubilate Group, available free on www.RESOUNDworship.org.

17 Keith Getty and Stuart Townend, available on www.gettymusic.com.

18 From London School of Theology, available from www.christianlifeand.com.

19 Available from www.licc.org.uk/bookshop.

20 Edwin Hatch (1835–1889), available www.jubilate.co.uk and in the book *Sing Glory* (Kevin Mayhew).

21 Noel Richards and Gerald Coates, © 1992 Thankyou Music, available on www.kingswaysongs.com.

Appendix 2

1 John L. Bell, © The Iona Community. In the book *Heaven Shall Not Wait* (Wild Goose Resource Group).

ENGAGEWORSHIP.ORG

Sam and Sara run *engageworship.org*—a new expression of the Music and Worship Foundation, furthering MWF's vision and values for a new generation. We aim to resource youth, young adults and 21st-century churches for innovative worship.

We want to help people engage with God, each other and the world around them, through creative, multisensory acts of worship. We are committed to excellence and breadth in music, but also exploring other forms of worship and creativity in church.

This goal is being achieved through a number of projects:

- Saturday training days: Focused on the needs of local churches and youth bands, these days aim to encourage you where you are strong, and train and equip you where you are weak, helping you to hold the tensions present in 21st-century worship leading.
- The development www.engageworship.org: A searchable creative worship database to give ideas for your services, plus articles and other training resources.
- Resourcing conferences and events: We are aiming to take people broader and deeper into all that worship can be, at events such as Spring Harvest, the Baptist Assembly and London School of Theology.

For more information, creative worship ideas and booking details, visit www.engageworship.org.

MASS CULTURE

THE INTERFACE OF EUCHARIST AND MISSION

ED. PETE WARD

Holy Communion... Eucharist... The Lord's Supper... Mass... each name has a different resonance, yet refers to the act of worship lying at the heart of Christianity. Church teaching may vary as to its exact significance but it remains, in one way or another, an encounter with the living God. How does it relate to contemporary developments in charismatic worship, Fresh Expressions and the emerging church?

In this book, ten contributors from a range of theological and church backgrounds consider the relationship between Holy Communion, mission and contemporary culture. This updated edition includes three new chapters, taking the debate further.

The contributors are Jonny Baker, Stephen Cottrell, Graham Cray, Stephen Burns, Ryan K. Bolger, Mike Riddell, Sam Richards, Dave Roberts, Martyn Layzell and Pete Ward.

ISBN 978 1 84101 580 4   £7.99
Available from your local Christian bookshop or, in case of difficulty, direct from BRF using the order form on page 143.

GROWING LEADERS

REFLECTIONS ON LEADERSHIP, LIFE AND JESUS

JAMES LAWRENCE

Seven out of ten Christian leaders feel overworked, four in ten suffer financial pressures, only two in ten have had management training, and 1500 give up their job over a ten-year period. At the same time, as financial restrictions affect the availability of full-time ministers, more people are needed for leadership roles in local congregations, for every area of church work.

This book faces the challenge of raising up new leaders and helping existing leaders to mature, using the model for growing leaders at the heart of the Arrow Leadership Programme, a ministry of the Church Pastoral Aid Society (CPAS). It comprehensively surveys leadership skills and styles, discerning our personal calling, avoiding the 'red zone' of stress, developing character, and living as part of the community of God's people.

ISBN 978 1 84101 246 9   £8.99
Available from your local Christian bookshop or, in case of difficulty, direct from BRF using the order form on page 143.

GROWING YOUNG LEADERS

A PRACTICAL GUIDE TO MENTORING TEENS

RUTH HASSALL

Being a teenager may well be more challenging today than at any time in recent years—and being a Christian teenager presents further challenges. Increasingly, the role of the mentor is being seen as key in helping young people to make right choices and learn to live well, so that they are equipped to find a safe path to maturity.

This book offers practical guidance to those who feel called to mentoring 13–18 year olds in a faith context, with a view to nurturing them towards leadership roles. Linked to CPAS's course *Growing Leaders—Youth Edition*, it also works as a stand-alone resource. It defines mentoring, analyses the necessary skills and attributes of a mentor today, encourages good practice, and above all considers how to help young people identify their gifts and grow as Christian disciples.

ISBN 978 1 84101 637 5 £7.99 (Published March 2009)
Available from your local Christian bookshop or, in case of difficulty, direct from BRF using the order form on page 143.

ORDERFORM

REF	TITLE	PRICE	QTY	TOTAL
580 4	Mass Culture	£7.99		
246 9	Growing Leaders	£8.99		
637 5	Growing Young Leaders	£7.99		

POSTAGE AND PACKING CHARGES				
Order value	UK	Europe	Surface	Air Mail
£7.00 & under	£1.25	£3.00	£3.50	£5.50
£7.10–£30.00	£2.25	£5.50	£6.50	£10.00
Over £30.00	FREE	prices on request		

Postage and packing	
Donation	
TOTAL	

Name _____ Account Number _____

Address _____

_____ Postcode _____

Telephone Number_____

Email _____

Payment by: ❏ Cheque ❏ Mastercard ❏ Visa ❏ Postal Order ❏ Maestro

Card no ☐☐☐☐ ☐☐☐☐ ☐☐☐☐ ☐☐☐☐ ☐☐☐

Valid from ☐☐☐☐ Expires ☐☐☐☐ Issue no. ☐☐☐

Security code* ☐☐☐ *Last 3 digits on the reverse of the card.
ESSENTIAL IN ORDER TO PROCESS YOUR ORDER Shaded boxes for Maestro use only

Signature _____ Date _____

All orders must be accompanied by the appropriate payment.

Please send your completed order form to:
BRF, 15 The Chambers, Vineyard, Abingdon OX14 3FE
Tel. 01865 319700 / Fax. 01865 319701 Email: enquiries@brf.org.uk

❏ Please send me further information about BRF publications.

Available from your local Christian bookshop.   BRF is a Registered Charity

brf

Resourcing your spiritual journey

through...

- Bible reading notes
- Books for Advent & Lent
- Books for Bible study and prayer
- Books to resource those working with under 11s in school, church and at home

- Quiet days and retreats
- Training for primary teachers and children's leaders
- Godly Play
- Barnabas RE Days

For more information, visit the **brf** website at **www.brf.org.uk**